D1130766

MONEY TALKS!

MONEY TALKS!

Charles Sopkin

RANDOM HOUSE • NEW YORK

FIRST PRINTING

© *Copyright, 1964, by Charles Sopkin*
© *1964, by Esquire, Inc.*

All rights reserved under International and Pan-American Copyright Conventions. Published in New York by Random House, Inc., and simultaneously in Toronto, Canada, by Random House of Canada, Limited.

Library of Congress Catalog Card Number: 64–14839

Design by Jeanette Young

MANUFACTURED IN THE UNITED STATES OF AMERICA

Contents

Introduction

I might have gone through life without really caring about millionaires had it not been for a magazine interview I had with one of them several years ago. The gentleman in question was colorful, caustic, entertaining—and he told lousy jokes. And he was an honest-to-God millionaire, right down to the gray-faced male secretary who was lurking around the hotel suite with an ample supply of hundred-dollar bills.

Frankly, I enjoyed the interview, and some weeks later, while looking over the material I had gathered, I wondered if it would be possible to write a book about millionaires which would avoid the blandness of the ghost-writer and the guile of the press agent. As you may know, a polite but firm paper curtain often separates the millionaire from his curious public. The result of this curtain is rather elementary: an endless series of speeches, articles, and books is published under the millionaire's name, and often they bear little resemblance to their authors. Vice-presidents in charge of public relations have a tendency to pamper and protect the hand that feeds them and the operational word driving everyone is "image." "But is it good for his image?" was the question that seemed to fall from most of the lips I talked to. It is not particularly easy to penetrate this paper curtain; nonetheless, my first millionaire (I have become fairly possessive about the men I questioned) intrigued me and I set out to see how many truly unvarnished interviews I could gather.

I was interested in how millionaires spoke, what they thought, how they made their money, and all of the other questions a reporter might want to ask a rich man. Moreover, I insisted that whatever the men might say be on the record, exactly as they said it. (There have been a painful number of "as told to" books published dealing with businessmen and millionaires, and every one of them has a polished but deadly tone. I didn't think there was a desperate need for another.)

I began with a list of two hundred fifty potential candidates, and gradually whittled this down to one hundred. Preliminary research left me with around twenty-five, on whom I did further research before actually undertaking interviews. I soon found that self-made men who founded their own companies gave much better interviews than men with inherited wealth. The self-made men of the mid-Twentieth Century possess an astonishing abundance of ego (and super-ego); thus the reader will find that most of the interviews in this book are confined to that variety. To my surprise, most of the men I finally interviewed agreed to be fully quoted. Basically, millionaires who have had their money for two or three generations don't want to talk to anybody about their fortunes. I also learned that men who had risen from office boy to president, no matter how self-made they might be, were often reluctant to talk frankly to me. Thirty years of service to a corporation tends to make anyone play it safe, especially the man who can't wear his Harvard Business School degree on his sleeve.

There was a tendency on my part to select the gaudier interviews for inclusion. My editor, who knows the nuances of "image" as well as anyone, prevailed upon me to keep the book as representative as possible. Therefore, the reader will find some pieces that will seem slightly unbelievable and others that sound pretty self-serving. I assure you, though, they all are authentic and untouched by ghostly hands.

Although most of the gentlemen in the book may strike the reader as utterly different, they do have a few things in common. All of my millionaires own a first-rate tax man, and one millionaire went so far as to install *his* accountant next door to his home for handy chats. All of my millionaires were touched, in one way or another, by the depression of the thirties—and the fear of another depression seems to be a driving force in their lives. All of my millionaires work seven days a week, and put in eighteen-hour days.

Several people who are festooned with degrees read portions of this book as it was being written and offered me reams of unsolicited comment. An eminent New York psychiatrist was delighted with the Freudian overtones of some of the interviews. A sociologist found that most of the millionaires pinpointed the "malady of materialism." A banker felt the pieces were fair; a Socialist said they were unfair.

I am impressed by these opinions, but I disagree with them. This book is simply a piece of journalism in which I have tried to avoid the handout, the glittering phrase, the touching anecdote (every good public-relations man has dozens of dramatic and/or heartwarming anecdotes), and all of the other impedimenta of our business community that separate a reporter from his subject.

–C. S.

New York City
October, 1963

MONEY TALKS!

I

In 1940, Wallace Johnson started building houses in Memphis, Tennessee, with $250 borrowed from a finance company. Today, at sixty-three, he is the president of sixty-eight corporations; he is one of the leading home builders in the nation; and he founded, along with Kemmons Wilson, the Holiday Inn chain of motels, which now number over 400 in the United States.

WALLACE JOHNSON

I talk to myself. Mrs. Johnson will confirm it, as will many of my friends. I've been doing it for years. For example, I used to smoke a lot; I used to smoke three or four packages a day. It was just one cigarette after another.

Then I read where a guy could make ten thousand dollars more a year without smoking and I just threw them down. But I bought me some cartons and I would lay them all over the desk everywhere and then I would talk to myself: "Wallace, listen, what are you going to do? Are you going to be a man or a mouse? So just don't smoke. It is self-control, that is the thing about it." And I quit smoking.

Other times I say other things to myself. "Wallace, I do not think your attitude was right yesterday. Let's straighten up that attitude. Let us see if you cannot show a little more personality, and a little more determination, with a little more understanding, with a little more thoughts of kindness."

Yes, I talk to myself, I ask myself what do I want. One of the major things that I do, I make a list of the things that I want to do. I mentioned this habit of mine in an article once and I am not ashamed of it. I also have copies of prayers that I have prayed for more than twenty-five years. One of my prayers was once published in the *Saturday Evening Post*. Another prayer I prayed in 1948 which was answered went like this:

O Lord make us one of the greatest leaders of the nation in the building of men and homes, and help the city officials of Memphis to understand that this is our goal, so they will help us instead of hinder us. Make me, O Lord, one of the leading Baptists and teach me how to win souls. O Lord, help me to be one of the biggest businessmen in the United States, and if it be Thy will, let me be a vice-president of the National Home Builders' Association.

God, please, oh, please, let us build two thousand units this year, and if it be in accordance with Thy divine purpose, let us accumulate two hundred and fifty thousand dollars in cash during that time. O Lord, help us to build a good house cheaper than anyone else in the United States. Help us to get lumber, or sawmills, or whatever else we need. May we be able to house the Negro citizens of our community as they have never been housed before. And, God, please, oh, please, help us to make connection with the right kind of banks, that understand that mortgages on Negro property are as safe an investment as any other kind, so that we can go on and on and on. Amen.

Lots of times young people ask me how to start out today. I once met with a senior class from the School of Business Administration of Ole Miss down at Oxford, Mississippi, and they asked me how to get ahead. I'll tell you what I told them. Times are a little different today than when I started out. I think that the man without a college education today would have a tougher, harder time than I did.

I also think there is a greater need today of the ability to think than when I came along. Assuming that you have a college education, the first thing that I would like to be possessed with if *I* were starting out in a career would be the proper attitude. The attitude to get the facts of anything. Most of us make the mistake by not getting all the facts before we make our decision.

And I would have to say as I have said to many of my friends, and sons of my friends, wives, and others, that a good business to get into would be the home-building business and the real estate business. I would say to any young man, Go into the building business and start from the bottom, being able to do any and all parts of it. How can you tell a man how to lay brick if you have not laid a few bricks yourself? How can you tell someone how to do something you have not done yourself? How do you know whether that is the right way to do it? How do you know what price to pay for your materials? Yes sir, if I had me some money saved up, I would take this money and I would go into the building business and I would go into the real estate business.

I would go where the people are. There are eleven states in the United States that have most of the population and money. Basically, you have got the Eastern part of the country. That is where the people are and where the money is today. It takes both combined—people and money.

If I were starting out fresh today, I would pick myself out a state and a city and I would go to a city—not a big city, but a smaller city because it will turn to a bigger city. Let's take Oak Park, Illinois, just out a ways from Chicago, Illinois. Let's take Gary, Indiana. Let's take Peoria, Illinois, where there is heavy industry. You can go out from Columbus, Ohio, where they have wads of industry there. Columbus, Ohio, is a fabulous, growing city. Boston and up in that part—well, they have not changed quite as fast as these other places. They are still talking about their history, not their future. This is still no discredit to Boston, because I have a lot of very wonderful friends there. But your opportunities to build houses are greater in Peoria than in Boston. Now that is where you can get the best good out of your money. Secondly, I would strongly urge the young man starting out to try talking to himself, as I am going to do here. I am putting myself up before the mirror and I am going to start talking to Wallace.

"Okay, Wallace, this is what you want to do, son. You want to go up to one of those cities and you want to find you some small acres or tracts of ground and buy it, with the least of an amount of cash that you can get, on the longest terms, with no interest, with the greatest release clause, so that you can actually start a subdivision or a development. Yes sir. You know the reason why you do not get more types of terms, Wallace? Because you don't ask for it!

"Wallace, do not be afraid of a debt. Do not be afraid of a debt. Be sure that you can do it, but do not be afraid of it. If you've got, say, ten thousand dollars saved up, Wallace, you're only going to buy a few lots. You're going to buy one or two lots and take an option on twenty more of them. And that option isn't going to cost you anything if you work it right. By saying it this way. The buying of two lots will give you an option on ten more. It can be done.

"Here's the way it's going to work, Wallace. You're going to buy those two lots for cash. You're going to take your ten thousand dollars and put it in the bank, and then spend five thousand dollars on the two lots, leaving the other five thousand dollars in the bank.

"Wallace, you're going to try and build a house that the average workman can pay for. Make the monthly payments about that of the average week payday of the people who are buying. Then you won't get all the low or all the high. You can catch it in the middle.

"I would leave that five thousand dollars on deposit in the bank and say to Mr. Banker, 'Now I have five thousand dollars on deposit and two lots out here. I have the take-out commitment from the Federal Housing Authority, so on this I want to borrow from you twenty thousand dollars.' I am going to keep my five thousand dollars on deposit always, and I will only use this twenty thousand dollars on the labor and material for my two houses.

"Good gracious, Wallace, you don't want a contractor

to build those houses! You're going to build and sell them yourself. You're going to hire the brickmasons and the other labor. You've got to be the contractor. You've got to be right there on the job to see what is going on. And you're going to sell your house at a fair price and whittle yourself out a twenty-five hundred dollar profit on each one of those houses that you're going to build for ten thousand dollars apiece. Be sure that you come out with twenty-five hundred dollars profit apiece on each house. And build them in about ninety days. Therefore, at the end of ninety days you're going to have fifteen thousand dollars—twenty-five hundred on each of your two houses and your original ten thousand you started with.

"This is where you're going to move, Wallace. You can take that fifteen thousand dollars and go forth and not build two more, but four more houses. And at the end of another ninety days you're going to have ten thousand dollars profit from your second batch, plus the profit of five thousand from the first two houses. So therefore you have your original ten thousand of your savings, five thousand and then ten thousand in profit.

"Now out of that you will have to take your living expenses, but live cheap. Man, eat hamburgers in place of steak! Don't let your first five thousand dollars go to your head, Wallace. Be honest in yourself and be a poor man and by jingoes when you get your first ten thousand dollars you will be richer.

"Build your house—sell it. Take that money, Wallace, and start selling and building those houses. Sell it yourself, but be sure that you have a profit in that house. When you get your profit, build you some more. Just keep it step by step. Keep climbing the ladder. Build it and sell it. From the sample of the house, Wallace, try to make as many pre-sells as you can. Sell to the guy for the house to be delivered. See? You are taking the risk out of it, Wallace. Be sure that you have a profit in that house before you start it. The profit is made in the design of the house. And knowing the cost in the house, Wallace, before you start it.

"From that step on you're just going to keep stepping up in volume, increasing your volume, increasing your profit, and watch the trend of the territory and look at your competitors. Wallace, the best thing for you to do, son, is to find out if the other man has a better house for less money than you do. If he does, then you change your house to where *you* have a better house for less money.

"I would like to say to you, Wallace, that the people that you sell your houses to can be your greatest servants. I would say to you, Wallace, know that family personally. Know who they are, where they work, where they go to church, and make friends with them. Then visit them and ask them if they can give you the name of some other people that might buy a house, and then you go to see them. I would say to you, Wallace, run ads in the paper —tell the people you want to buy real estate, you want to develop real estate, you want to borrow money. It really takes money to go along with it. And when you find that piece of property, or that real estate, have faith in your judgment. One of the things, Wallace, that you need to do is to believe in your decisions at all times.

"And Wallace, know that with God's help you can make that profit off that piece of real estate come as a way that you would like for it to be. Be sure that you hire people who want to work for you, who will do a good job and sell your house while working with them. Be sure that you are honest with those people. Do not think that you can make a hundred thousand dollars without them knowing it. If you make profits rightly divide a percentage of it with those people that helped you to make it.

"When you hire a man, hire his wife, too. Interview his wife at the same time. This is an important thing to see that the wife will be happy if John stays out working late at night. Ask this John Doe to give you suggestions on how you can take your business and how you can do a better job of it. Ask every employee on the job what he can suggest to you to do a better job other than what you are doing. As you continue to grow, tell the story, but be honest when you tell it. Tell your story to the people that can be told and helpful to you.

"Tell it to bankers, to the title company, to the news-papers and to the real-estate men. Get up and get other people bragging on you as soon as you can. Hambone said he could brag without lying, therefore let him brag. Get someone else to bragging on you. *Sell* this other guy to bragging on you.

"Then, Wallace, as you go on up the ladder with your profits, you buy a few more lots, a few more pieces of real estate, find you a girl to marry. Wallace, if you are not married at the age of twenty-five, you had better get you a wife right away that can really help you. You be sure that you love this girl and that she loves you. You tell her every day that you love her and she will tell you that, too. She will be the greatest partner for you; she will help you count the money; if she is the right girl she will help you build your business. She will encourage you when you become discouraged. So you be sure that you have your partner along with you there, but be sure that you have first of all God as your partner. I would suggest to you, Wallace, that you have faith in God, that you write your prayers of exactly what you want, and keep a record of it. God keeps a record on you. Why don't you keep a record on Him? You will be amazed at the answer you will get. You ought to just try it and see what you will see."

From the scorecard I have just given, anyone with a lot of sense could become a home builder. The easy thing for me to say would be to follow my career and by golly you'd be a rip-roaring success by the time you're forty. But my story might be a little different to the average person since I almost was forty years old before I started in business for myself. I was born in Mississippi and started out as a carpenter and I was determined when I was fourteen years old that I was going to be a contractor. In that day, people were known not as builders but as contractors. So you always took a contract to build houses for different people. And at the age of sixteen, I started out being a full-fledged carpenter. At eighteen I had made eighteen hundred dollars as a carpenter.

I made that eighteen hundred dollars by working hard at the profession. I started studying engineering and carpentering from Radford's Estimating book. I made that money working with my own hands. That's a lot of money to save. I worked for it and I made it. I picked cotton when I was seven years old, so I have been working ever since I hit this earth. At the age of twenty, two years later, I had lost my eighteen hundred dollars. I was four hundred dollars in debt and I lacked two years of finishing high school.

What had happened was I saw a mantle in a building magazine, and I thought I might like to put it in this house I was building for a railroad agent down in Mississippi. I sold this guy this mantle, which happened to be in demand in a few places around the United States. So, at the time I went to install the mantle I had run out of money and I didn't have any money to pay the brick-mason to lay the bricks to put the mantle up, so I had to do it myself.

I mean I had to literally put it up myself about six times before it would fit together. This type mantle was a design of scenery and trees; it was just beautiful scenery, all within this mantlepiece. If you missed the wrong limb on the wrong tree, you just had to start all over. Even though there was a design, by the time I got through working with it, I had worn the design out and had forgotten how to put it together. I finally finished the house and found myself lacking two years of finishing high school.

My mother and a professor talked me into going back to high school. I had to go to school twenty-four straight months, and not miss a day. It was a pretty hard thing to do at the age of twenty. The kids in school gave me a hard way to go but I was determined to do it, so I went through high school and finished up. About two months after I finished high school I was approached by a man who asked me if I wanted to go and run a retail lumber yard in Mississippi. I had never been a manager of a retail lumber yard in my life, but I knew how to estimate, knew how to build, lay brick, and everything else. I was determined that I could do everything regarding the construction of any house.

Before I took that job I had been jerking sodas in a drugstore. While I was there I met the future Mrs. Johnson, and one day I asked her if she would marry this big boy. She said yes. So I went to the drugstore's competitor, Mr. Stevens across the street, and borrowed eighty-five dollars so I could get married. I was twenty-four years old when I got married.

I got married on a Sunday, at ten o'clock, and at two o'clock I went to the lumber yards and fed the mules. And then I went to work on the next Monday morning at the lumber yard. We've just had one big long honeymoon for thirty-eight years. Then the Depression came along. The banks were all closed and things fell to pieces.

I had been at the lumber yard for a little over four years when the crash came. Things fell out over the whole country and there was nothing else to do down in Mississippi, so I came to Memphis. I put an ad in the *Commercial Appeal* and I described myself to the best of my ability. I called myself a good estimator, a draftsman, a house builder, a contractor, a salesman, and I got a job in Memphis through the mail.

So I came to Memphis and went to work but the Depression kept getting worse and it just really got terrible. Then I left Memphis and went to Pine Bluff, Arkansas, to go to work at a sawmill there. The only time I was ever fired in my life was in Arkansas. I had coffee with the superintendent that morning at ten o'clock in his home, and at eleven-thirty he sent a note up to the sawmill which said upon receipt of this note you are fired. They sent the note up there and Mrs. Johnson brought it up there by the side of the yard. After this guy sent the note he got into his car and left.

My wife took a look at that note and, why, her little heart was just breaking. I mean for a guy to get kicked in the seat of the pants that much was really rough. I have never been able to understand why the manager of the sawmill was so nice to me and then fired me. It has always been a great mystery to me and it taught me a great deal. It was a great lesson. It showed me that you can never fully understand human nature. That is something that you have to watch, but then you still do not even know the answer to it.

I got fired in 1936 and went to work in Jonesboro, Arkansas. Meantime, I had put another ad in the Memphis *Commercial Appeal.* I described myself from the top to the bottom just like I did in my first ad. And I got a letter from a man who wrote: "If this is the Wallace Johnson that worked for us five years ago, report for duty Monday morning." That is how he answered the ad. I had been working in Jonesboro for two days when I received this letter. So I quit on the spot and came down to Memphis on a Saturday. We stayed at the Chisca Hotel in a three-fifty room.

I think the total cash money my wife and myself had at that time was possibly twenty-five dollars. The next morning Alma said to me, "Sweetheart, do you have the purse with the money?"

"No, you have it," I said. So, we turned that room upside down and couldn't find it. I didn't wait for the elevator. I went down five or six flights of stairs out to the car to look to see if I could find the purse. Our car was a two-door '35 Ford. I combed through that car and I couldn't find it at all.

The combined cash in my pocket at that time along with Mrs. Johnson's cash amounted to fifty cents. Out of gas, no breakfast, and our money gone. We went downstairs again and got into the car. Why, I was so nervous I could hardly stand still. I also had an appointment with this man I was supposed to see about the job. As I was getting into the car I turned the seat down for Mrs. Johnson to get in. That purse dropped into the floor of the car. It had spent the night in that car. We picked it up with tears in our eyes and drove halfway out Union Avenue before either of us could say anything to the other. It had been a very tense moment, and we were just that upset. We drove on past this man's house in order to clear up a little, and then went into his house to meet him. And he asked me if I could go to work, and I said yes. So, I came over and went to work. I had been working for this lumber company for three years, making thirty-seven fifty a week when I decided to go into business for myself. I worked with them until December 1, 1939, and then went in and told them I was going to quit.

I was right at forty years old when I went into business for myself. But still I had in mind all these number of years of not doing anything but being a contractor. Mrs. Johnson had nothing in her mind but being an interior decorator. So, every book that we could find on building, estimating, construction, detailing, we just both of us would spend the time with them.

Now, how did I go into business for myself? I borrowed

two hundred fifty dollars. I had no cash; I had less than twenty dollars. I borrowed this two hundred fifty dollars on this Ford car. I borrowed the money from one of these lending companies. And I went in business for myself with this borrowed money. That winter of 1940 was undoubtedly one of the coldest winters ever to hit Memphis. It was the only time to my knowledge that the Mississippi River froze over.

The first house that I built was at 132 South McKellar. It started to freezing and raining. It really was a rough time. I was more than sixty days getting the foundation laid. It was a rough job. The roughest job I ever had. All I had for living money was that two hundred fifty dollars and I didn't know a guy could buy a nickel's worth of beans, and meat, and make it go that far, but you can. We just saved our money and lived off it. I was able to get F.H.A. insurance on that house I was building and I was able to talk a bank into financing it. I had sold it before I built it and that first house I built, I made one hundred eighty-one dollars off of it. Then I really started to building. But in the meantime to get started, I needed more financing. I talked to different companies I would be associated with into waiving to a first mortgage. In other words, they said to the finance company, We have so much faith and confidence in Wallace Johnson that we will see that you get your money first and then we will get ours. What they did was to waive their lien rights in favor of a first mortgage. I was one of the first ones to do speculative building: that would be to build without having sold first. In 1940, I built a hundred and eighty-one houses. But here is something else. There was a world of people to watch me, so I had a printer to print me up some pasteboard signs that said: "Let Wallace E. Johnson Build Your Home on This Lot." They cost me about a half a cent apiece. Then I bought five dollars' worth of paraffin wax. I would dip the signs into this wax so that they could stand up under the weather. I had five thousand of those things made and I put them up all over the city. I just put the signs on the lots—and remember I didn't own any of those lots, either.

I was up at the bank one day making a five-dollar deposit and a real estate man here in town was making a deposit and he said, "Where in the world did this Wallace Johnson come from? He owns more lots in town than any other one man. I never saw a man that owned as many lots in my life. The very idea!"

I didn't even own a one of them. I didn't ask the guy if I could put the signs up. Why, heck, I just went all over town and put the signs up on everybody's lots. I mean I just put them all over the whole of Shelby County. I had Mrs. Johnson at that time answering the phone at the house. The idea was that if somebody did want to have a house built on a lot where he saw a sign, why, I would then go out and buy the lot—and I usually was able to.

We were still living in the same two-bedroom apartment we got when we moved to Memphis, paying forty-five dollars a month rent. I still had my Ford car, but I had to pay twenty-five dollars a month to keep it. And I was still working on that loan. That Christmas of 1940 we decorated a house as a Christmas present. We put a big red ribbon around it with a Santa Claus on top of it, and put on a sales program. The results were about thirty houses sold.

Business started off with such a bang that I had to hire

some people. Mrs. Johnson to begin with was keeping the books and answering the telephone. We started to set up our office in the living room of the apartment. After three months we had to take one of the bedrooms for office space and before we moved out we had offices in every room in the apartment. We did our sleeping in one corner of an office. Then, Mrs. Johnson was looking after the decorating and I was looking after the buying and building.

At one time in 1941, I had thirty-two unsold houses on my hands. That is a large number of unsold houses. The bankers had said to me, "Wallace, unless you can reduce your inventory we will not be able to keep going with you." So, I called the carpenters, the paperhangers, their wives, the whole gang together. I gave them a Coca-Cola at this meeting and I said: "Co-workers, listen to this closely. I am handing to each of you a list of houses we have on hand that are not sold. Now, unless we sell them you will not have a job. We tried, we've run our ads, but we haven't sold them. So I want every one of you to talk about it at the drugstore, the grocery store, the service station, the church, or wherever you go." We planned, we worked on it, and within two weeks' time every house was sold. And we never moved out of our office. Those carpenters, bricklayers, and painters sold every house for us. I didn't give them a commission. It was either that or no job.

I have always treated my people right. For instance, on a lot of the jobs the foreman was always cussing the carpenters and painters and common labor and it was just unbelievable how they would cuss the people. I said we were not going to have one bit of that on our jobs. That man is a human being with a heart, with a soul, and we are not going to have it. At no time have we ever allowed the foreman to cuss at any workman on the job in any shape, form or fashion. I have many times dressed up as a carpenter and gone downtown and mingled with the workmen and asked these fellows whether they were happy working for Wallace Johnson.

The first year I was in business for myself I cleared about twenty thousand dollars. I was working about eighteen hours a day, six days a week. We always had Sundays off. We would work up until twelve o'clock Saturday night, go to Sunday School, and start right back to work Monday morning. In 1941, I said I would turn out a house a day, sold and finished. I made it. Built and sold three hundred and sixty-five houses that year. Everyone was working. Mrs. Johnson and myself were just going and going at all times. I was also buying land, developing land, building on land.

I have been building houses and such ever since. In some of the years I have turned out as many as two or three thousand houses. I don't know how many houses I have built in all. I have not counted for the reason I didn't really want to put the number out. I in turn would feel that I was bragging. This is what you have to watch out for. So many people want to put you in the category of a big shot. If I were to tell you how many thousands of houses we've built for the public, you would think I'm bragging on myself. Whatever success that my partner Kemmons Wilson and myself may have had it never registers with us. Even all those houses we built never registered. Nor does the fact that Mrs. Johnson and I own sixty-eight corporations make any impression either.

The only bragging I do on myself is only with the most important thing on this earth—my body. When I get in an airplane and I'm going to do some aerial surveying of land I say to that pilot, "Listen buddy. I am more important than all the rest of you. I want a safe landing. This is an important body that I have got, I love myself, very definitely." I started picking up all those corporations during the war when business really began building. It was the fact of business that the ninety per cent tax on profits would require me to do it. I started to separate my business into different corporations, and I would come out better doing it that way.

Back in 1951 I built a motel and I called it Bomah Motel. (I had a club in my organization known as "Bomah" —Builders of Men and Homes.) But I sold it. Anyhow, I knew something about the motel business. Kemmons Wilson had built the first Holiday Inn in the year 1952. One night in 1953 at a meeting of the Home Builders, Kemmons Wilson, who I knew as a big builder of houses in Memphis, came over to me and said that he wanted me to come in with him and be a partner on Holiday Inns. Kemmons wanted to put Holiday Inns across the nation. I sent out seventy-five letters to builders across the nation. Sixty-eight of them showed up here. Kemmons and I tried to sell them on the idea of Holiday Inns; they were supposed to go out and build a motel and get a Holiday Inn franchise. After the selling there were only three of these builders who went along with it. Even though we romanced them, and sold them, they didn't go. At that time I guess maybe we two boys had from three to five hundred thousand dollars each invested in it. And both of us were pretty well scratched for cash.

Things got so bad at one point Barney McCool, who is Mrs. Johnson's brother, didn't even have enough traveling money to go out and sell franchises for Holiday Inns. But Mrs. Johnson had some cash and she gave Barney fifteen hundred dollars. He took that fifteen hundred and went out and worked and then came back for another two thousand. He took the check and I didn't even know it because we owed so many bills and we were just up against a brick wall. I can tell you that I did a lot of praying during those days.

Of course the rest of the Holiday Inns story is so much history. My partner Kemmons Wilson is one of America's greatest men. He will never speak an unkind word about a living man. He will never repeat a bad story about a living man. He will only sing praise or he will not sing at all. This ability of Kemmons had helped us to become the world's largest chain of motels. There are now more than three hundred Holiday Inns in the country, and new ones are popping up every day.

But the most important thing of all to remember is that you can make money from anything. About three years ago a man came into my office and wanted to borrow some money from us—he put up some land as security. Later on, we bought the four thousand one hundred acres of land from the man which included some abandoned rice land which was ideal for a lake. So we filled up a few acres and made a nice lake out of it. Then a man told us we ought to go into the catfish business. So we put sixty thousand catfish in there. Then another guy came along and told us we ought to go into the bullfrog business. So we stocked the lake with six thousand tadpoles and six pair of bullfrogs along with the catfish. Then we put up lights around the lake and at night when these lights are on the bugs flock to the lake and the frogs feed on the bugs and I guess the catfish feed on the frogs. We should make a good profit off the catfish pretty soon.

One last thing I got to say to all this. You've got to learn about people first and foremost if you're going to be a success. For instance, I watch a man's eyes. I watch him when we are talking. A man can talk back with those eyes, and you can tell whether you are making an impression on him or not. Remember, each one of us has acres of plantations upstairs. God was smart when he made a man. He made four holes in his head for information to go in and made only one for it to come out. So, you watch the features to see what is happening with what you are saying. If when talking with a man and he does not stay with you with his eyes, he will probably not stay with the subject you are talking about. Those are the things that I notice.

One of the great reasons that people fail to succeed is because they do not know themselves and they are not honest with themselves. We are what our thoughts are. During the course of years I think that Mrs. Johnson and myself are what our thoughts have been. It is just that simple; this life of yours is just like an empty field. Your mind doesn't care what you plant in it. You can plant rice, or corn, or cotton in the fields down here on earth and that ground doesn't give a dad blame what you planted. But, whatever you plant, you fertilize it, and that is what grows. Now this mind of yours is the same thing. If you plant wrong attitudes, wrong thoughts, that you married the wrong gal, or got the wrong job, these are the things that will grow in your mind. But if you plant the things like, "Man, look how lucky I am, just look at me," then you can have a good attitude and that will grow with you forever and forever.

II

William P. Lear, Sr., decided at age sixty that he wanted to go into the jet plane business. He sold out his holdings in Lear, Inc., an electronics concern, and flew off to Geneva to develop his plane. Recently, he decided that he would be better off producing his plane in this country, so he moved his entire factory back to Wichita, Kansas, where he now is engaged in building jets.

WILLIAM P. LEAR, Sr.

Now if I was just interested in making money, I would go down and I would buy every piece of property that I could buy in Athens because Athens will be another Acapulco. In ten years from today, a piece of property that you can buy in Athens will be worth from ten to a hundred times as much and I don't give a damn where you buy it in Athens.

The best thing that the average guy who's plodding along in his job can do is to buy a piece of property. One of the best ways in which almost anyone can be rich in his youth is to just go out and buy a piece of property someplace. It would be almost impossible for him to find a piece of property that he can buy today that won't be worth much more when he's twenty years older. You know why? There will always be more people, but there will never be more land. So therefore the price of land has to be directly in proportion to the number of people. Now if a man's smart enough to buy land in some place where there's going to be a greater growth, a greater usefulness for the land, then his increase will even be greater. I could show any man today with a very limited amount of money how he could increase the amount of his money to ten to twenty times over a period of ten years.

The thing to remember when buying property in certain places in the world is that you have to be able to have hindsight, not foresight. All you have to do is look and say, "Well, this happened in this area and the conditions for that happening in *this* area are exactly the same, so therefore it's got to happen in this area, too." For instance, Europe today is the classic example of the one place in the world where you can operate with hindsight and people later on will say, "You have the greatest foresight in the world." Well, why is that?

Because what is happening in the United States today will happen in Europe tomorrow, so if it's already happened, if it's already successful in the United States today all you have to do is pick it up and take it over there. Take such things as soft ice cream. In some parts of the U.S. it's called Frost, I think. Anyhow, it's a tremendous success here. You take it over there; it's going to be a tremendous success there. This thing works both ways. Look how successful European sports cars became over here.

But this hindsight thing works much better when regarding Europe. There's an enormous increase in the standard of living in Europe today and this increase is what you have to watch. When we had the same rise in the standard of living in America, note what it was that went on here and what made the big successes and then transplant it to Europe. Now where else in the world can you operate with hindsight as your means of determining what you should do in the future? You can't in the United States. I can point out one thing after another to you. For instance, the supermarkets are beginning to take hold like nobody's business. I went to Europe five or six years ago and they said, "We're not worried about the increased use of cars, we've got our autobahns and so forth." And I said, "But those autobahns are going to be positively the most dangerous things you can be on in the future. It won't be long before they'll be packed with cars."

So the Europeans said to me, "No, this will never happen. All the people use bicycles here. We don't have many automobiles." Now it's a risk of your life to go one hundred miles on the autobahns because the cars are bumper to bumper and you just know that it had to happen. You could see that all of the factors were increasing the standard of living. Also, it meant that they were going to have automobiles. In America, we have two cars—one in the garage and one sitting out in front of the house. Ten years from now, they'll have television sets, radio sets, frozen fruits, just about everything.

Now going back to property, I think it's ridiculous to try to pinpoint one specific spot in the United States where you can buy property that will go up in value. It can't be done. Instead, I'd buy land around airports. There's been a tremendous boom in jet travel and more and more airports have expanded, and are being modernized. Any land around these airports has to go up in value. To show you how correct this kind of thinking is I went to California and I saw a piece of property for sale at the Santa Monica airport for a hundred thousand dollars. I bought it and everybody said, "Well, that sure was a stupid idea. That property had a city deed on it a few years ago and the total worth of it was twenty-seven hundred dollars." But I went ahead and paid one hundred thousand dollars. I sold it only because I was forced to sell it. I had held it for about six years. And the S.E.C. forced me to sell it because when my old company, Lear, Inc., went on the Big Board I couldn't own the property and lease it to my own company. This is the rule of the S.E.C. So I sold it for five hundred fifty thousand dollars and this is after keeping it for only six years. See? Now it will be worth five million in another ten years, so I didn't have any desire to sell it.

When Grand Rapids wanted to put in a new runway they—the county—didn't have the money to buy it. I suggested to the county that I would pay for the part of the property that they didn't need for the runway. I offered to pay the cost of all the property they had to condemn if they would give me back half of it. They did. We paid a total of five hundred dollars an acre for that. To show you what can happen to property around an airport, we sometime later had to buy some more of the same property and that time we had to pay seven thousand dollars an acre. And it was worth every penny.

Lots of people wonder, if they're starting a business, whether they should go in hock to get the business started. I'd say it depends on how intelligent a fellow is. If he is really sure about his business, he should mortgage his house. I've mortgaged everything at times to stay in business. As a matter of fact, I can remember a time when it seemed I owed everybody in the country. There are few ways to be successful if you haven't got courage, unless you marry money or are born with it.

I don't think children should start from scratch, but they won't be terribly happy if they get too much of their money by inheritance. My kids feel it's unfortunate to be pointed out as rich kids. The reason some people are wealthy and many aren't is dependent upon many things. "Nothing risked, nothing gained" may make the difference. Intelligent, calculated risk is the first principle of investment gain. Hard work, confidence and spirit applied to a useful task are mandatory.

When I sold my stock in Lear, Inc., for a sizable amount, I could have taken it easy for the rest of my life. Instead, I'm now investing my time and money in my latest project, the Lear Jet Corporation. I'm betting that there's going to be a tremendous market for an efficient jet aircraft for executives, a plane that will keep up with the big jets. Better than that, I'm relishing the problems, the challenge and joy of doing something useful, creating a product to meet a real need.

I'm counting on my analysis that there's going to be a growing market for such a jet. I've got the courage to back my convictions—with my fortune! In fact, I think it's going to be a great success.

First one needs the ability to anticipate a market for something, then the will to struggle and find the product to fulfill that market, then the courage to put your money into its development.

Many people have wonderful ideas of how to make something, but they're not successful for the reason that they have a "dime museum" type of invention. It doesn't have a place in the market. It's a great idea, but nobody wants it. You've got to produce a product or deliver a service people need and will want to buy.

One time when I was busted flat I became frustrated and frantic and considered foolish and futile solutions. But then I said to myself, "Wait a minute. Calm down. All you have to do is figure out something that the world needs and make it." I figured that the world right then needed an all-wave radio set that could be manufactured at a low price. Applying myself to the problem day and night for two weeks resulted in perfecting an idea that I sold for a substantial amount. Flat busted in the morning of Friday, the thirteenth of April, and well off by the thirteenth hour of that lucky day. Note that instead of whining and decrying my fate, I found something that the world needed, made it and sold it.

The formula for personal success is the same now as it always was. Perhaps a little bit more difficult, because of governmental requirements for so many forms to be filled out. It's harder to start a small organization. Today you not only have to meet the payroll but also make withholding deductions, fill out the forms, send in the tax, along with everything that's connected with government—forms, licenses, etc. This makes it more difficult for a young man starting a business today, especially if he's going to employ more than three people. When I started out, all you had to do was make the things that were wanted.

Despite these tedious and extra details, the opportunities today are just as great. Some of my friends right now are starting a little concern, and I wouldn't be surprised but what that thing in a period of eight to ten years will be a substantial success that could easily be worth a few million dollars. Take a couple of my friends who had an idea for making instruments and aviation equipment. They're going to succeed first of all because they *are* a small company. Big companies eventually become inefficient.

They have built-in inertia and levels of management and can't move quickly. Occasionally from within these big, slow-footed companies, individuals with bright ideas decide to form their own company. Three or four fellows may get together, pool their money and say, "Now, we'll start a little company and run it on a shoestring until we prove what we want to do." Obviously they burn a lot of midnight oil and get a lot done, compared to what they would do during easy hours in a bigger organization, where a workday is for a specified period and there's no overtime and where things are done by system.

So this little company of entrepreneurs chisel some things and use some second-hand stuff to get going and soon have a system functioning. If they're working on something that was really needed, they'll generally find a limited market for it and reach the point of incorporating and perhaps selling a few shares of stock.

The principal thing most of them do wrong is selling out too early in their effort to get money into their organization. A stock broker will propose a stock offering to raise five hundred thousand dollars and these guys say, "This is absolutely great. Now we'll have all the money in the world to work with!" They forget that when they're getting this five hundred thousand dollars they're going to end up with only fifteen per cent ownership in the company at that stage of the game. If they would hold on longer and suffer a bit longer and work more midnight hours they might be able to get five hundred thousand dollars for, let's say, fifty per cent of the company. But if they held on two, five, or ten years, that stock in their company grows, because of their original effort, their intelligence, their hard work, and that stock could easily be worth a million dollars to each of them.

Now about these midnight efforts: I think there's evidence of a growing decadence in the U.S. today. Look at the history of Carthage. The Carthaginians became so swamped with spare time that finally there was no longer a Carthage. Discussions of three-and-a-half and four-day work weeks have gotten to the point where in the end people won't be working at all.

Once I said, "If I ever catch anyone going to the washroom on his coffee break, I'd give him one hundred thousand dollars." Originally that's what the coffee break was supposed to be. Now they go to the washroom on your time.

Add all this up and you find that possibly one of the great needs of industry today is to have a work break. We've got to begin rolling up our sleeves and going to work. This hypothetical group of fellows who started their own little company have no problem in the beginning in getting them to put in twelve and fourteen and eighteen hours a day. Why? Because their heart is where their treasure is and their treasure is tied up in this little business which will go down the drain if they don't work that hard. All they have is a little handhold, which they can make into something if they put in the extra effort and intelligence to convert their idea into a reality of some kind—a mechanism, a device, a computer.

It really isn't work. I don't think anyone can work around the clock as I do or as others who are building a business do, just for the money involved. You have to have something more than that. You have to be tremendously interested in what you're doing. Sure, expectation of profit—but that isn't the main reason. Take the fellows I was talking about. They probably would have had plenty of security and money by staying in the organization from which they splintered off. But they're so eager to get their idea developed that the hours go by without their knowing it. This is the fundamental necessity for the success of a splinter group.

Now if the splinter group becomes successful, it will be built into a big company. Ironically, it eventually will have all the built-in inertia and tangled management as to encourage some other group to splinter off and start another small company in the hope of getting something done. This is healthy. There is probably an economic law that works like this: when a company reaches a certain point in bigness it loses its ability for fast footwork unless the guiding light of the company is willing to keep his fingers in every project. If it gets too big, the guiding light can't keep up with it; therefore the company does get inertia.

I would say a young man has a better chance if he has an idea for a service. He won't require any machinery to execute his idea. For instance, there's a radio station in California that became virtually an overnight success. What do you think it specializes in? News. Nothing but news. Twenty-four hours a day. They were smart. They said, We'll specialize in news bulletins, news breaks, elaborations of news, repetition of news, and whenever we get a commercial we'll let them have only half a minute and it's got to be good. This station goes on and on to an exceptionally enthusiastic audience. Get in your car and the first thing you do is turn on the news. This is a classic example of an idea that made the grade.

You don't have to have a product. The radio station was a service. It's the only thing they have: a service to listeners. And I'll bet it was some young fellows from another broadcasting organization who got an idea that they tried to sell to twenty-five or thirty different people who said, "It'll never go." Somehow they got the money to put their little station on the air. Now everybody thinks, "That would have been a great idea. Why didn't I think of that?"

You see, the opportunity is still there. Probably when those fellows sell out that radio station eventually, each of them will be rich. The only way in which anyone can become rich any more is on the basis of capital gains. You can't do it just on earnings, regardless of how much salary you have, because ninety-one per cent is taken away from you in taxes. Some day they may straighten out the inequities in the tax situation, but the minute the capital gains situation is taken away from us, that minute you're going to see the end of opportunities for people to become rich by their own effort and ingenuity.

Even though there are still opportunities today, I'd rather have started out when I did, in the pre-red-tape era. When I was eighteen years old I started a company to make model airplanes. We ended up making radio sets. My partner and I were kids who had a good business idea but didn't make any money because we didn't know how to manufacture. It points up the fact that I always had a motivation toward producing something that has a market.

My first job was working as an assistant in the power station owned by a leather-tanning company. I was just sixteen and had the problem of starting up the power station at six o'clock in the morning from the low-power generators to the high-power generators. As soon as I could do the whole job I no longer had any interest in it whatever, so I quit. You couldn't have got me back no matter what you paid me. That was the history of my early job experiences: as soon as I became the best there was in a particular situation, I completely lost interest in it.

Then I went to work for International Rotary in Chicago, as office boy for their Secretary Emeritus, around 1919 or 1920. As office boy, I sat in the corner and listened to one of the most astute and educated men with whom I have ever come in contact. As he dictated letters and articles I learned a little about language and its use because I kept my ears open. Later there was an opportunity to go into the Multigraph department, and I worked up from being a type cleaner and paper sorter to becoming head of the department at one hundred sixty dollars a month, when I immediately lost interest and quit the job.

Around this time the U.S. Air Mail was coming in at Grant Park, and I went to work for nothing as a grease monkey so I could be near airplanes. My mother was going to have me committed at that time for leaving a job where I was making money and going to work for nothing. I couldn't get any place in the aviation business then, as it was either get out or work for nothing, and I needed money. So I went to work for Western Union, operating a typewriter.

A minute ago I was talking about language. I'd say one of the most important things of my life was learning how to speak better. I learned some of it in Rotary. I also learned it in church, listening to Paul Rader, an evangelist. I listened to him all day Sunday—morning, afternoon, and evening. He used language beautifully. Remember now, I had only a grammar school education and was a real Chicago "deese, dem 'n' doze" boy. I guess anyone could still detect a lot of Chicagoese in my pronunciation, but listening to Paul Rader helped me a lot. It is a tremendous advantage to be able to express yourself well when you have to sell an idea or a product. You ought to be able to handle language and handle it easily and fluently. So listening to Rader did me enormous good. First of all, it showed me that there was a way of talking that was expressive. This was something I hadn't known, but afterward I kept my ears open and learned how to do it by repetition.

I never learned grammar. I don't know anything about

it. This is one of my difficulties in learning French, because I can't distinguish between a verb, an adjective, and an infinitive. People who learn languages by being able to take it apart are much better off, especially in learning a foreign language. Today it's necessary to know how to use language. I didn't have to go to college to get it; I just had to keep my ears open.

I have quit many jobs in my time. When a man gets to the top of a particular job he should either ask for a more difficult job or get out and find another, even though the new job may not be on a higher level than the previous one. The thing that counts is gaining a new element of learning from the new job. There's nothing I ever learned on a job that I haven't used at some time of my life. For instance, once I was a storage battery boy. What I learned then has helped me enormously when I have needed to know about storage batteries.

In designing my new jet airplane, I found I could back the engine-maker's engineers right off the board because they were making a false assumption that changed the weight of the airplane by one hundred fifty pounds. I was able to save this precious weight on the plane because one day a long time ago I happened to have a job that taught me all about storage batteries.

I think worrying about fringe benefits is bad. It's definitely bad because this anxiety over security is the basic thing undermining our whole American way of life. It can destroy our way of life. People have such a yearning to be secure that they're willing to sell out all the things our forefathers bought with insecurity that made their security. Security isn't worth that much. They should be secure by virtue of their abilities, their ability to cope with things, rather than relying on the built-in security, we'll say, of a governmental agency. This is pitiful to see.

I had a man working for me as chief engineer right after the war. I wanted to keep him and asked him what he wanted most. He said, "I want security," and I told him I would try to see that he had it. The company was reorganizing and putting out some stock that would be worth enormously more in the future. I asked him how much money he had, and when he said about fourteen thousand dollars I said, "You go out and buy fourteen thousand dollars' worth of our stock right now," knowing it would increase in value. He bought the stock and within some three months it was worth about a hundred and fifty thousand dollars.

Six months or so later I said to him, "Okay, now you've sold back your stock and are worth around one hundred and fifty thousand. Now that I've provided for your security, I hope you're happy?" He said, "Well, Mr. Lear, just the reverse is true." I asked "Why? What do you mean?" He said, "I could never be secure with a company that could make money for me that fast." So he quit and went to work for another company. He felt very insecure with me.

He wasn't the only insecure guy I've ever had working with me. Once a very stupid situation came up ten or eleven years ago when one of our bookkeepers came in to me and said that the company was broke and there was nothing left for us but to call the sheriff to come and take over the company. I said, "Listen, I can remember when I owed everyone, banks and creditors, and didn't have a dime in my pocket, but I never felt it was time for the sheriff to take over the business. Here we have a million eight hundred thousand dollars in government securities. We have a one to two ratio between our payables and receivables and you say we're broke. You're out of your mind!"

We came out of that thing smelling like a rose. He had been worried because he couldn't see that the money we were borrowing was going to make money. If I hadn't borrowed money and kept going on all of these situations, we'd just have folded up. This is just a case of courage.

Those are the fundamentals, then. Nobody is going to make it based on earnings. A man has to earn something to get a nest egg. This is very important. Then he must invest in something that is going to increase in value and try his darndest to pyramid that. When he buys something he has to be sure it is going to increase in value. He's not going to sell, because he will get only a small increase in value. You see, at one time I could have sold a half interest in Lear, Incorporated, for fifty thousand dollars. I sold out for several millions. You have to believe in what you're doing and not merely take a quick profit and run. You have to stick with it and work. And you have to have courage. Courage. Boy, do you have to have courage!

III

*J. J. Mascuch is the founder
and president of Breeze Corporations, Inc., of Union,
New Jersey, and Victory Engineering Company, of
Springfield, New Jersey. He has been an inventor for
more than fifty years and holds one hundred fifty
patents in the automotive, aeronautical, and aerospace fields.*

J. J. MASCUCH

I was born on June 2, 1896, in Newark, New
Jersey, on Montgomery Street, opposite Krueger's Brewery.
My father had been born in Slovakia and my mother in
what is today called Czechoslovakia. They migrated to
this country when they were young, met in Trenton, got
married, and had a family of ten children. There are two
survivors of the ten children today—my brother, who is an
engineer, and myself. My sister died a couple of years ago
while I was on a safari in Africa.

We lived in a neighborhood that was composed mainly
of Irish, Germans, and Jews. It was not a tough neighborhood. The people were mostly religious. My father was a

patternmaker and he specialized in designing locks for prisons and various foreign governments and particularly the railroads and the oil companies. He worked at this trade for some fifty years. After school and on weekends, I used to go down to the factory and help him assemble locks and learn the principles of machine-shop practices. I had a desire to use my hands and was mechanically inclined. This is where I got some of my inventive genius, if I may term it as such. I guess I was around twelve years old at the time.

If I made a mistake while working for my father, I got a belt. When I wasn't working for my father, I worked for a butcher in the community, selling and taking orders for meats and groceries in a suburb of Newark. When I was thirteen, I spent my spare time in a garage helping mechanics repair motors, changing spark plugs, magnetos, and did some odd jobs around the garage any time I had a chance. It was there I developed a yen to build. They had some old motorcycle engines around and I took some spare wheels, built a chassis out of oak wood, put some springs on it, and built a little car, which I completed at the age of fourteen. It took me over a year in my spare time to build. My father thought it was too expensive for my blood. The men around the garage helped me to get parts and made some of the castings for me and some of the forgings I needed. Then I developed a friction-type clutch that gave me a variable speed from zero, and a maximum speed backward and forward without any changing of gears.

Don't think that little car came easy. I had to put forth a lot of effort and in the early days I made a lot of mistakes because I was rather on the timid side and was too bashful to ask questions. Had I to do it over again, I would have asked more questions and I would have cut the building time in half. I could go around fifteen miles an hour with the car. I rode it all over the neighborhood. I was warned by a policeman that I couldn't ride on the street because I couldn't get a license. There was no ordinance for it, so I used to drive it around the sidewalks. A lot of people were curious about the car. They would stop me and talk to me about it. Some of the people felt sorry for me and every once in a while I told them I needed a part. I would do a little begging and they would give me some money to buy a new bicycle chain or a new part.

All the time I was going to high school I was meeting people and if they needed anything fixed, or if they needed any chores done, I always helped out. I would get tips and this built up my bank account to the point where I could go out and buy electric motors and second-hand batteries, and ignition wire and switches. I built a little steam engine, and then a large-scale plane that flew. I was getting up at four in the morning to go to work for the butcher, and I was going to school six or seven hours a day. Sometimes I used to get into a battle with my parents who wanted me to go to bed early and rest. In those days I was a skinny kid so I built myself a milk-shaker with an electric motor and put it on the wall. I used to make myself milkshakes with a little cognac and sugar, and this eventually built up my constitution.

I was seventeen when I graduated from high school. I wanted to go to an engineering college where I could further my experiences and studies and back myself up with a basic education. I realized then that without an education you were lost. So I worked in a tool shop during the day doing a lot of drafting and designing and went to Newark Engineering College five nights a week studying engineering. It took me five years to get the degree and for five years I never missed a night. I made about nine dollars a week during the day at the tool shop.

Then I went to work for Hyatt Roller Bearing as a designing engineer for Alfred P. Sloan, Junior, who later became head of General Motors. I was designing journal boxes for railroad cars at the age of nineteen and I was also going out on service calls. Mr. Sloan took a liking to me and I didn't think anything of it at the time. The reason he took a liking to me probably was because there were extra chores to do and I never was a clock watcher. If I had to work extra hours to get something out, I worked.

I was making a hundred and fifty dollars a month, which was very good money at the time. Then I heard that the company might be sold to General Motors. So I had six hundred dollars in the bank I had saved up and I bought Hyatt Roller Bearing stock for less than a dollar a share. I think I put up less than a hundred dollars and then I paid the rest over a period of time. I got close to a thousand shares for my money. Within a year, General Motors bought out the company and they swapped something like two for one. To make a long story short, that original stock that I got in General Motors which is selling better than seventy dollars a share, and which has split many, many times, cost me around thirty-seven or forty cents a share.

I have been a stockholder in General Motors for over forty years. It has taught me to buy a security and never sell it. "Never sell" has been my philosophy for half a century. Then I bought ten shares of Christiana Securities. That was the holding company that "held" General Motors and the Du Ponts owned a big block of it. I was nineteen, I think, and I paid six hundred dollars a share and I only had to put up ten per cent of the cash to make the purchase. I borrowed the money from my parents. It sold a couple of years ago for fifteen thousand dollars a share. It then split eighty-five for one, so the stock that cost me six thousand dollars is worth I guess about a hundred and fifty thousand. I keep it now as a token investment and that's about all.

I had been in the National Guard, but when the First World War started I got myself transferred to the Air Force. I was twenty-one and I trained in gunnery and aerial observation in France. I had about eleven thousand dollars in stock at that time, in G.M. and Christiana. At first I was an artillery officer and I was not quite twenty-two when I started flying. I was wounded in the back of the neck one morning during observation of artillery fire over the German lines. I was wounded about six o'clock in the morning and back on the firing line about eight-thirty. I had a machine gun, but this fellow came out of the sun and dove at me. We flew Spads. They were simply bamboo and canvas. There was no protection to the pilot until the Second World War. Even then the American planes didn't carry any armor and it wasn't until the Jap Zeroes got on the tail of our planes and killed our tail-gunners that our American government woke up and said we have to put armor on. Hell, I knew we needed armor in 1918.

A lot of our boys got hit in the back and legs. So I

started stealing metal plates out of French racing cars. In fact, whenever I could get a piece of steel I grabbed it to put under my behind so I wouldn't get wounded. As a result of my ingenuity, I developed armor plate which our government eventually adopted. Those planes were made of bamboo, ash spars, covered with linen, doped with shellac and everything else. That's why when they were hit they would go up in flames in a minute.

When the Armistice was signed, I was stationed in Tours, and they asked for volunteers to become members of the Peace Mission in Paris. I applied, took a preliminary examination and I became a junior member of the Peace Mission in Paris with a diplomatic passport and so forth. I had a good time working for the Peace Mission. I traveled all around Europe with a chauffeur and everything. In my travels I met some very noble people and I met all kinds of con men and I met people fleeing the end of the Russian Revolution. I even got a chance to visit a Turkish harem.

When I got out of the service and finished with the Peace Mission I came home and opened up a laboratory. The first inventions that I produced were mostly for automobiles. I developed the shielded spark plug. I made them at night and went out and sold them in the daytime. In the meantime, I was working on spark-plug cleaners. I worked on automobile bumpers. I worked on radiator caps. I worked on transmissions. I built the hammered piston ring which was a cast-iron piston ring and hammered under a special process to make it hard on the outside, so it would cling to the wall of the cylinder.

I was getting patents and eventually I sold them out to

people and would get a royalty on them. Then I would take the proceeds of this to make other inventions. I made money partially on my inventions and also on investments on securities. The market was rising and I was associated with financial people and was following their advice about investments. In 1929, when I was worth about six or seven million dollars, the market collapsed and I was almost wiped out. Well, I wasn't wiped out completely. I just wasn't as rich. I probably wound up with a million bucks or so. I paid off all my debts, and never had to go through receivership. And I still had my lab. That's when I started pushing radio shielding for airplane spark plugs, and this has become standard equipment on airlines all over the world.

Things kept on building. We sprang from probably a dozen people in the lab and got much bigger and then I bought two or three companies and merged them. And then I invented rust-proof bumpers. The first thing you must remember about inventions is that you've got to find out whether there's a market for the device that you have, and whether the device is useful or not. So what did I do? I made a sample set of bumpers, put them on my Lincoln automobile, and I took just one trip to Boston. I sold six hundred thousand dollars' worth of bumpers on that one trip and then got a manufacturing company to start making them.

I want to keep repeating the thought that it isn't tough to be an inventor even though it might sound like it is. First, you've got to have the stick-to-it-iveness when you work on an invention. The invention has to be new and novel. Now a lot of those people who *think* they're in-

ventors don't go anywhere and they die poor. Very seldom
do you find a combination like myself, who has engineering ability and executive selling ability and also inventive
ability. This came through the hard knocks of life. The
measure of your trials and tribulations is a measure of your
success, not the measure of your pocketbook. You've just
got to stick to it. Luck is what you make it. People say,
"Oh, he had a little luck. He's a lucky so-and-so." Like me.
They say I'm lucky. I'm not lucky. You just have to work
and you get a lot of disappointments and you've got to try
them all over again.

A lot of people today make the mistake of calling some
things inventions which are merely improvements on an
existing invention. I've developed a new type of bottle cap
which will probably revolutionize the bottling industry.
This is an improvement on an existing invention. On the
other hand, my radio-shield spark plugs were entirely new
and a pure invention. In other cases, people have invented
something which is new but which hasn't a bit of practical
use. It might generate the greatest imagination of the
individual who developed it, but perhaps the fellow is a
little premature.

He may be five years ahead of his time. If you invent
enough things, though, you're bound to develop some
good ones. But you've got to be thinking all the time.
What has helped me enormously has been my travels
throughout the world. I saw the need for inventions in
every country I visited. I saw the need for different types
of belts and conveyors, for safety devices of every descrip-
tion. One of the products that my company Breeze is
working on is called the Breeze Grasshopper. We're sub-

mitting this to the military. It's a self-catapulting device to carry one or two soldiers with attack weapons over small hills and streams or gulches. The Grasshopper moves in leaps of one hundred and fifty feet. It can take troops into places that can't be reached by ordinary vehicles. We got the idea for the Grasshopper by watching a giraffe leap in Africa. I was on a safari actually on a vacation, but I turned the trip into something very useful when I got the idea for the Grasshopper by watching the giraffe leap around.

You've got to have an imaginative mind to be an inventor. You've got to be an original thinker. You've got to have at least average intelligence. But you don't have to be brilliant or a genius to be an inventor. When you get into complex mathematics and science like inertial guidance, then you've got to be brilliant. But you have to keep in mind always what your invention is going to do. For instance, there was a tremendous demand for my shielded spark plugs in an airplane so that ignition interference was eliminated. There was a need for the first rust-proof bumper for cars, see? I did a lot of things first that were new and useful.

The big need today for inventions is safety gadgets. Anything to promote safety is needed. This is a tremendous field. Anything to promote safety and anything that promotes health. The big field now is electronics and medicine. I'm working on a thermometer now that records the temperature of the individual in three seconds, instead of three minutes. To record temperature in the hospital with the conventional thermometer costs forty-six cents. With this electronic thermometer I'm developing, as fast as you can touch the man's body you can record the temperature. And it's much cheaper.

To become an inventor you also must develop your personality. Usually you're born with a good personality. If you develop your personality people will begin to like you and they will make certain disclosures to you that normally they wouldn't make to other people. They'll talk about their innermost secrets of life, their family problems. They'll also reveal to you whether they've had accidents in the home, or whether they've ever been burned in the home. Then you absorb this information and if you can make a better mousetrap than anybody else, the people will buy it. Any kind of safety thing around the house is good. For example, somebody ought to notice that there are a lot of serious burns when infants pull hot coffee pots on themselves. So if somebody could come up with something that could prevent a hot coffee pot from tipping over he'd have himself a pretty good item.

You know what else is needed? A separate compartment in the medicine cabinet to keep the kids from going into them and getting into trouble with drugs. It would keep all medicine away from children. You could make it a separate compartment that would be transparent and you might have a little lock on there so the kids couldn't open it. And you could cement the whole thing right into the wall of the bathroom or to the base of the medicine cabinet. You wouldn't have to worry about standardizing the size because they make medicine cabinets of all sizes today. Now I don't think I'd call this an invention. It's really an improvement on an existing product.

If I had more time to fool around with things, why, I'd

try to do something to make drivers keep their minds on the road so they wouldn't be gabbing all the time and miss signs. This is what causes a lot of accidents. I would try to make a device that could go into every automobile that would automatically knock off your ignition, or retard your speed, like a control, if you exceeded the speed limit. Were two cars to meet at an intersection, the control would govern their speeds so they couldn't seriously damage each other.

There are safety gadgets that are needed that people can use around swimming pools. Swimming pools are becoming more popular, even more popular than golf courses. There are a lot of things you could come up with, like making the perimeter of a pool out of ordinary cement and putting emery dust into it to keep you from slipping when it's wet. I don't think any company has done exactly that kind of thing. When I painted the deck of my boat we used a lacquer. I put emery dust into it, and the emery dust acted as a file and you didn't slip all over the place. You could do the same thing around house pools, also around the home. If you wanted to, I'll bet you I could sit down and figure out a way to make a tile with an abrasive in it so you wouldn't slip and break your neck whenever there was water on the kitchen or bathroom floors.

If the ordinary man applies himself, it is very possible for him to invent something. Definitely possible. But he must believe in what he is doing, have real interest in the invention and never delude himself about its success. The only time I ever failed at anything is when I gave up the idea. I have never failed if I stuck to it and I have stuck to some of my inventions for several years before they came to fruition. They come to you as an idea and then it's work, research and more work, and that's the real road to success. And what is success? It isn't money. It's the satisfaction of doing things for mankind.

Most people run into trouble with inventions because they don't know where to go with it or what to do with it. Sometimes their idea looks so juvenile that the average person who thought it up is afraid to discuss it because he feels that people will ridicule him. My experience has always been different. When I had an idea, I went to the garage mechanic, I went to the boss. I asked their advice. If there wasn't a boss to give me the information, I went somewhere else, or I went to a doctor, or a lawyer, and I kept on asking until I got the answer or the right direction. Sometimes I thought I got the correct direction, but it would be wrong and I made a mistake. Then I'd start all over again. So you've got to have a yen to develop and make these things. Now, Thomas Edison was a good friend of mine. He was a very careless individual and I don't say this to take anything away from him. I think he was a wonderful man, but in fact he didn't have the respect of a lot of men that worked for him. When he issued an order, he used to write it on such things as sandpaper or on the back of an old letter. But the reason that he made such wonderful successes is because he had faith and never gave up. Too bad that Edison died virtually a poor man.

When you figure you got something that people will want to buy, you first have to make a reduction to practice —that is, a model. It doesn't necessarily have to be to scale, or even work perfectly. After you've built your model, you then go to a patent attorney and you take out a patent application. Your patent attorney makes regular patent drawings. Then it is filed with the U.S. Patent Office in Washington, and they give you a serial number. Once a patent has been accepted as filed, you have what is called an early filing date. Anybody who comes up with a similar idea doesn't have a Chinaman's chance. You were the first one.

As a rule, I always carry a pencil and paper with me. All my life I've done this for taking notes. You can never remember all the points of an idea no matter how good your memory is. You'll miss something if you rely on your memory, but if you write your thoughts down on a piece of paper you can review them each night before you close your eyes and go to sleep. You can make a personal inventory of your good ideas and your bad ideas and see what to keep or discard. I've done this for fifty years. I've got every idea of mine down on paper. Just remember, an invention is usually developed from an idea that the individual is interested in. For instance, the average inventor could not invent a catgut that is used in hospital work, or a machine that administers anaesthesia, because he has no knowledge of it.

If you invent something, you should go door to door pushing doorbells trying to sell it. And you'll find when you're selling that the consumer will tell you how to improve your product. After you've tested the product then you can go to any company or any individual who is willing to put up the money to go into production.

Most of the people who are angels and put up money for inventors see their money go down the drain because either the invention's no good, or too premature. There are always a lot of these angels around. They're like theater angels. They all want to make more money and they think they can make a million dollars on your invention. And that all depends on what the invention is.

Any time a person wants to show me an invention I always see him. I don't have what I call "crackpots" calling on me, but I do have people calling on me who are emotionally unstable and who suffer from what I call an obsessional neurosis. They get an obsession about an idea they might have and nothing can change them. But I always see them, talk to them, and encourage them. Sometimes I give them a couple of hundred bucks. I have a colored fellow that comes in every now and then to see me. He says he's got "perpetual motion." He comes in with all these tubes that take the water and pass it from one vessel to the other. Now if he knew the first principle of kinetic energy, see, and dynamic forces and balances, see, and what friction means, he'd know the lousy thing wouldn't work, but I, Joe Mascuch, should educate him? If I told him what was really what, do you know what would happen?

He'd go out of that office and probably say, "That son of a bitch. He wants to steal my invention." See? So I encourage him. Never discourage a guy. You've got to give them the oil in that case. I used to get myself in a wringer many times by being honest with guys, you know, telling them what I think. It just doesn't work. If I've got a friend and his wife is running around and I know about it and I tell my friend, "Look, we've been friends for years and I hate to say it but your wife is running around. . . ." Why, he'd hate my guts for it.

When you know these kind of things, don't tell anybody. Keep them to yourself. Never tell anybody that. Never let the left hand know what the right hand is doing. You can't do it. But as long as there is greed and sex on earth, you'll always have problems. Read the papers. It's only sex and greed. I do a lot of work with psychologists, and I know quite a few good ones. They agree with me about sex and greed. The mind has a lot to do with the individual, and your mind is molded by the company you keep.

There's a lot of trouble today in business that leads to the biggest bunch of thieves in the United States. Greed working again. I heard of one chemist who works for a big oil company. His bosses think that this guy is the greatest in the world. This guy in the meantime is getting around a hundred thousand dollars a year, but he's also siphoning things through the back door to someone else. This is a scientific thief. That's worse than a guy going in and holding up a bank with a toy gun. And this scientific stealing is very common. It's a very common practice indeed. And they say this guy has won many big scientific prizes for his work. That guy is mentally sick, I say. He needs psychotherapy.

I'm in the ninety per cent tax bracket. I have to make three hundred thousand dollars a year just to put the key in the front door of my house. It costs me thirty thousand a year to live in my house and that is very conservative in the way of an estimate. I don't object to paying the taxes, but I couldn't call it a "privilege." I think this is one way, through our new philosophies, that the government will confiscate the income of the people. Only here we call it taxes. They want to centralize everything, see, and when you get to the point where they take the initiative away from the individual, we will become a decadent race that can't compete with the Europeans.

I think this business of catering to the individual from the cradle to the grave is a great disaster for our democracy and the things we once stood for. This is the wrong philosophy. Today, it looks like the balance of political power rests with the unions, the investment trusts, and the pension funds. And if it continues they'll control the funds of this country in the very near future. Then some strong man who doesn't care for his political career will have to come along to save us. Teddy Roosevelt used "The Big Stick" and took the balance of political power away from the big railroads, the banking fraternity, and the oil companies and gave it back to the American people where it belonged.

Now a "big stick" is necessary the way our labor unions are growing. I don't begrudge anyone making a living if he works hard and if he's willing to work. But to keep people on the payroll for not working and encourage them to go on unemployment at a fifty-dollar-a-week dole is absolutely pathetic. This is the trouble with our country. We are not producing and therefore we're losing our gold. I think the dollar is going to be devaluated and the price of gold has got to go up.

We can't compete that way. I don't care whether we pay the man five dollars an hour if he gave us five dollars' worth of work. But why pay him five dollars an hour when he gives two dollars' worth of work?

A man should be permitted to run his business like he

did years ago, without any fandangled government regulations. This is the trouble with the country today. So why should a fellow like me, or anybody else, knock his brains out and wind up with no more money at the end of the year? There's no reward. When men made money in the old days they kept a great portion of that money and reinvested it in new ventures that made new jobs. This doesn't exist today.

And this talk of going on a three- to four-day week is silly. A man would be moonlighting and have two jobs. I estimate that I work an average of twelve to fifteen hours a day, seven days a week. Despite all these problems, I do think the opportunities afforded today in the space age are greater than they ever were. But one of the things I object to in this country is that a man with two or three kids has a real money problem if he wants to send them through college. And any man who is a citizen in the United States should be given the privilege of educating his children. What we ought to do is to allow the costs of college to be taken off the income tax as a full deduction. If this country can find money to give to Europeans we should first do this for our own people and let parents send their children through school and take it as a full tax deduction.

We should do this because children are the wealth of our country. We must count on our educated people. Russia is doing that and is creeping up on us. For every scientist and engineer we produce, they produce three. It's just like having one factory with ten people and the other with thirty people—both making the same stuff. Which do you think is going to produce more and better?

Everything in life is attitude. If you get nervous and you

don't get enough sleep, you'll only fatigue yourself. If you smoke or drink too much you can't function at anything very well. You've got to get your rest. You've got to take a vacation once in a while, so you don't go stale or have a nervous breakdown. Actually, people like scientists who get heart attacks don't get them from physical condition as much as from frustrations. The reason I know this is because I am associated with a lot of professionals doing electronic medicine.

Now I'm approaching seventy years of age and I still can do things that I did when I was thirty. Calisthenics. I dress on one foot. I put my socks on with one foot up in the air. I tie my shoes on one foot and balance myself. I actually can walk a tightrope today at my age. This all comes from practice and experience. Ice skate, ski—I can do any kind of sport. I am a good horseman. I can saddle a Western bronco and then ride him. It doesn't bother me.

If I had another professional career, I would have become a doctor, I think. But not like the average doctor today. Your average doctor does not have the time to care for his patients because he's so clogged up with his daily routine in the office. He doesn't have any time to do any thinking for himself, see? If I had been a doctor I would have been a good one because I am good with my hands and I'm not afraid to operate, or anything else, see? One thing good about being an inventor—it can lead to many other things. For instance, my inventions led me to my business. And then the inventions made the business grow. And now the growth of my businesses has led me to the biggest business of all—the aerospace industry.

I don't have any hobbies, as such. The whole world is

my hobby, so to speak. For example, I bought a Rolls Royce several years ago for fifty thousand plus. Then I started to tinker with it. I sent it over to Italy and had those fine Italian coachmakers put an entire new body on the Rolls. I had a toilet installed in the back seat, and a television set, and I had the windshield made with a special tinted glass I developed. So you see, I get my relaxation in many ways.

But I'll tell you honestly the thing that really worries me is the attitude of the people of this country. We shouldn't dilly-dally. We should be strong. We should not let the communists push us around. We shouldn't trade with them. This is my belief. I think our President is a good President, but he's making a terrific mistake in not having a bigger stick. That's all I got to say except you've got to remember in inventions that necessity is the mother of any invention. And you've got to give a little, take a little. Believe it or not, don't try to take it all with you. Give some of it away. That's basically the way I think.

IV

Carole Stupell is the owner and operator of a highly successful, extremely expensive gift shop on Fifty-seventh Street in Manhattan, where you can spend up to $10,000 for a set of dinnerware if you are so disposed. She has been in the table-setting line for more than thirty years.

CAROLE STUPELL

I work hard because it's necessary to do it. There's a lot of work to be done and that's all there is to it. I'm usually in my store at seven-thirty or eight in the morning and end up around eight at night. Long before this, I used to work up to two or three in the morning. The work just doesn't get done unless you do it yourself. I generally work seven days a week. Of course, it depends upon whether you consider this work. I wonder whether I'd be happy without doing what I'm doing. In other words, I doubt it very much whether I would put in these hours if I didn't like my work. I love what I do. I get a kick out of what I'm doing. And there is always so much to be done, and that can still be done. There just aren't enough hours in the day to accomplish everything.

The reason I come in very early in the morning and on Sundays is that I'm not interrupted. During the day, it's almost impossible for me to concentrate. In years past I've had very competent people whom I could delegate work to; unfortunately, I can't seem to find those people today. I was a secretary many, many years ago and I can type faster than my fastest secretary. There are certain peaks in my business when I'm just inundated and I probably consider the business a hardship but on the whole, I don't, when I analyze it. The most picayune detail—I love to do it. I love to do it in a manner that is quicker or better than it was done previously. I get a kick out of that—I feel almost like an efficiency expert. I like to see the quickest way that a thing can be done.

I don't make any distinctions about the different qualities of men or women in business. I don't think there's a difference. I have had men in my organization who were very, very excellent, and I've had women who were very, very good, too. Even in the artistic end there are plenty of men who are creators and designers. If you're good, you're good. Male or female, there is no difference. I don't think success in business is preserved for men only. I don't think sex has any part of it.

What I will say is this: There are a lot of women who have creative ability and good backgrounds, and good education, who have lived well and who have an innate sense of good taste. These are the women who have something to offer and they should utilize their abilities instead of planning bridge games or going to matinées. The woman who has this kind of discriminating taste invariably can do something that would be profitable. Also, I think this woman would find a great deal of pleasure in business if she did go into it. Unfortunately, women just don't do it. Those who are well off—financially well off—don't bother doing it. But they would enjoy it if they once got into the field. Of course, if a woman starts out with a small business which suddenly grows and if she's doing better than her husband financially then this can lead to an impasse.

Yes, it is a problem. It could develop into a very serious problem. I am married. My husband was in the theater, but he left the theater and became a marvelous helpmate to me. He switched from the theater into business and now he is the one who handles the operation of our office. I think it all depends on the individual. On one hand, the husband can be very proud of his successful wife and I think an individual should be given credit whether that person is male or female. Again, I don't think sex enters into it. I feel that people will recognize one's ability. It isn't as though they're both in the same business. I think if a woman starts her own little business that her husband would be very proud of her.

That concept of a woman's place is in the home is very much out of date. I think, of course, that it all depends if you can get good, competent help. There are many people who still maintain an excellent home relationship with their children and their husbands and their business doesn't interfere. What is the difference if you're in business or you spend most of your time in the theater, or out with the girls, or what have you?

I've been in business for myself since 1929. I was an assistant buyer in one of the large department stores in New York City. I was always very aggressive. I always wanted to learn a great deal and my buyer felt I was trying to get her job, which was not at all true. I just wanted to learn as much about that particular department as I could. So, she went to the powers that be and I was fired. Well, I had always had a yen for merchandising so I went into business for myself and opened a gift shop. I had lost some money in the stock market and I was in debt and I didn't have a dime to my name at the time. But I usually could sell—a bill of goods, my ability, anything. And fortunately I had the good sense to go into the Barclay Hotel, which was one of the better locations in New York.

I opened in December and everything was payable on January first: rent, manufacturers, merchandise. I knew the volume of business that I would have to do in the month of December and I also knew that if the volume was O.K. my immediate needs would be taken care of. I kept my fingers crossed and that's how I opened up my first store. I did my own decorating and I opened on practically nothing. I had no problem with those first bills. The December volume was fine and I never had a problem. I wasn't nervous at all. I had a great deal of confidence in what I could do.

As you know, all of this was in the era of Prohibition and about a year later a funny thing happened. I don't drink at all and I had no knowledge of hard liquor but I knew that in the hotel many of the guests would be coming into my shop for glasses. So I thought we'd better get some of those in. I went to a manufacturer and he started to tell me about wine glasses, and port glasses, and highball glasses, and shot glasses, and so forth. He was called to the phone and I looked around and discovered a rather interesting shaped glass. When he came back I said I'd like to have eight of them and he became hysterical. When I asked him what was so funny, he told me they weren't glasses, they were vases. But that didn't bother me. I just loved the shape of it. Anyhow, I put the eight vases on display and we sold them in an hour. Then I ordered two dozen, and they went in a hurry. In a short period of time I was ordering a hundred dozen at a clip. And that was the introduction of the Zombie glass. If you recall, the Zombie was a very tall drink.

I had no help and we were open from nine in the morning until eleven at night. You see, we'd get the theater people returning to the hotel. Of course, I had to get in very early to unpack my cases in the hall and bring the things in. And also in the morning I did my own deliveries. This was the only way to save money, and I had to save somewhere, naturally. I can't recall how I did that first year except I only know that to me credit was the most important thing in the world. I knew that if I was going to be successful, I'd have to establish credit and when my bills came due on the tenth, they were paid. If I had to go without eating, my bills were still paid on the tenth of the month. That still holds true today. That's the number one item that is paramount in the success of my business.

After the first year, I was asked by the people in Southampton to open up a branch out there. So I closed up the Barclay shop for the summer—during the summer months in New York it's very quiet—and I opened in Southampton. My place was called the Cocktail Shop. We did very well in Southampton since we had all the Social Register people from the Hamptons. One woman had a great deal of influence on me when I learned that she liked to use brandy snifters for water glasses. That gave me the feeling that people can be individualists. You don't have to be run-of-the-mill.

I was in the Barclay for three years, and then the shop got much too small, so we moved to 443 Madison Avenue, in the Weylin Hotel. This was in 1933 and since Prohibition had been repealed I changed the name back to Carole Stupell and took off "Cocktail Shop" because I knew that everybody and his brother would be opening shops featuring drinking accessories. We went into decorative appointments of china, glassware, and everything along those lines. I was in the Weylin for about five years and it finally got too small there, too, so we moved to 507 Madison Avenue. I was there for twenty-five years.

At 507 we had a great deal of floor space plus a huge basement and a mezzanine floor. Business was picking up every year. I was never satisfied. Let me say that—I am *never* satisfied. And yet, even now, I look around here and see so much that has to be done—so many things that I want to do. And there isn't enough time to do it.

Although I started out in the middle of the Depression, there was always money around. Even in Southampton, where the people were supposed to have been hit very hard, loads of money was being spent. You must remember that my customers had real wealth, and they had inherited a lot of money. These were the kind of clients we had because of our location. You see, everything I bought was in good taste and it was only a question of keeping up or ahead of the trends.

I made my annual trips to Europe in search of new and finer products. I went to California twice a year, and I was away a great deal of the time creating and designing. I was an important influence in the market in stressing co-ordinated table settings. It was back at the Weylin that I was amazed one day when, despite the fact that I carried china, glassware, linens, flatwear, all the appointments, I could not assemble one beautiful table setting for the window. And then it occurred to me that if I, who had so much of this material around, couldn't put together a beautiful table setting, how in the world could the average woman? That's when I decided, then and there, that everything I sold would have to be correlated—only I decided to use my own name and called it Carolated.

And over the years my judgment has been confirmed because most of my customers buy only Carolated table settings. At one time or another we've had all the important people. And of course two of my favorite people are the Duke and Duchess of Windsor. I sold to Grace Kelly and Haile Selassie, and the Armours, and the Fords, and the Aldriches, and the Du Ponts. You name them, and they've all been customers of mine. At one point we had a branch in Washington and we had the dollar-a-year men as customers, and Mrs. Roosevelt, and Perle Mesta, all of them. I closed the Washington branch in 1947. I was in Boston, too, but I had to close the operation because of lack of competent personnel.

Let me tell you something about the trouble you have

hiring people today. I see little children on the buses and I hear them talking and they sound so intelligent and I'm really amazed. I think children today are much more intelligent, but where are these bright young boys and girls when they come out of school? I have interviewed so many college graduates who have applied for jobs as administrative assistants that I am sick of it. Such incompetence! They're not really prepared. They have an academic education but you have to teach them the fundamentals of everything. I don't know. I can't understand it at all. I don't even bother advertising for assistants any more. The only people that I have found who ever developed are the people who started at the bottom. I can go on and on and on about this subject because it's the root of all evil in our day and age.

The evil that I'm talking about is simply this. These young people come out of school and they expect to start at the top. They have no knowledge, no background that is suited for the job. And then they want a high salary. If they had something to offer, you would be happy to pay—anything—to get competent help. I would. But they are not able to cope with the situation. They need training and experience, and you can't afford to pay this kind of salary while you're training someone. And you haven't the patience that you would have ordinarily if they started at the bottom. If they did start at the bottom, they would really amount to so much more and in the long run they would wind up with a much greater income.

I have started people off at a hundred and fifty dollars a week but I usually find they've sold me a bill of goods. So I get rid of them. And that's the reason there is such a high turnover. Furthermore, these applicants tell you they've got obligations—they've got their rent, they've got their children, or they have one thing and the other. No employer wants that responsibility. All the employer wants is for his or her employees to perform for whatever they're earning. Furthermore, today you've got unemployment insurance. The more people you hire and then let go for incompetence the more you've got to pay as your share of unemployment insurance. Therefore, you have to be fifty times more cautious not to hire people unless you really know they have something on the ball. I don't think I'm a difficult employer to work with if I think a person has intelligence. If I feel that a person *has* intelligence and doesn't live up to it, then I'm more annoyed than if the person didn't have any intelligence at all. I just can't tolerate incompetence.

Right now, I've been thinking about opening a branch in Palm Beach, and people have been begging me for years to open up in places like Rome, or Florence, but I just don't know. It gets back to that old problem of personnel. I could have become national without any trouble except that I don't know where I would have hired the people throughout the country. It is just as easy to buy for one store as it is to buy for fifty stores. For that matter, it's more difficult to buy for one than it is for fifty. I have been seriously considering franchising and yet, with my reputation, I am so afraid that the franchised departments would not have the personnel to have understanding and background and the ability to properly co-ordinate that it would do more harm than good to my reputation.

About five years ago I made up my mind to take it

easier because I had been working so very hard. And I had the idea that I only wanted to sell the table settings, completely Carolated, and no other way. It could run as high as ten thousand dollars a complete set, but you also could get a set for as little as two hundred and fifty. So, this was my dream. We had so much casual traffic on Madison Avenue. And I wanted to cut that out. I felt that on Fifty-seventh Street no one would *dare* walk into my store unless they really were potential buyers. It wouldn't be like the museum it was on Madison Avenue, with people walking in and gaping at the prices. But before I moved out of Madison Avenue I opened my Fifty-seventh Street store and ran both simultaneously so I could test my theory. We operated both stores for three years and when I saw that the Fifty-seventh Street store *could* operate on this basis I shut down the Madison Avenue one. And while a great deal of our sales are co-ordinated settings we still carry the individual items.

Once in a while I have a customer come in who will say, "I still love the china you sold me twenty-five years ago." Well, that's just too bad because I wish she didn't love it so much and she'd get another set. This is what I'm trying to do. I don't want people to buy one set and consider that's it. I have one customer on the West Coast who owns ninety-six complete table settings. She has one room on the top of her estate which was built especially for her table settings. When she has a dinner party, she simply tells her butler, "I want number thirty-three, or twenty-one." It's all catalogued for her, and she knows exactly how many place settings are in each one, the color, and so forth. That's the kind of customers we like.

I don't think this is excessive, not if it gives a woman a great deal of pleasure and if she does so much entertaining. This is her life. She really loves it. I have quite a few customers in Texas who have any number of sets. I don't say a person has to have ninety-six sets of table settings, but I should think they ought to have at least six changes. And I don't advocate that they have a dozen place settings in each set, but only as many as that person expects to entertain.

Although some people think it's silly, I firmly believe that the proper table setting can help eliminate juvenile delinquency. You see, the table is actually the meeting place in the home. That's the one time of day when the entire family is assembled. The dining table is the time and the place to get acquainted. If the children are exposed to a beautiful table setting they will know that time and attention are being given to them, not just to strangers. This will have a profound effect on the children. For the rest of their lives they will appreciate the affection and the attention that this represents to them. A beautiful table setting should not be done just to impress strangers. The immediate family comes first, because it implies to the children that their parents love them and they are getting the attention they deserve.

When you talk about someone going into business for themselves, you've got to talk about good taste. There is no question that the movies, the magazines—all the periodicals, in fact—have had a great deal to do with the development of better taste. At times I feel we have come a long way in the matter of good taste. Designs are much better now, but you still have a lot of manufacturers who are dragging their feet. Sometimes when I go to the gift shows, or the lamp shows, I believe the designers must have had ice cream and pickles the night before. I have never seen such monstrous stuff. It's the manufacturers' fault. They are not helping to develop or encourage good taste. It is also true with the ready-to-wear industry. Some of the garments that are being shown are fantastically bad. Apparently their attitude is that change, no matter if it's good, bad, or indifferent, is always a stimulus for business —and who cares, as long as it makes money.

Let me go on record as saying that there is always a place for a person who has the ability and the willingness to work. There is no such thing as being out of a job. There is always room. Everybody is looking for people who are willing to work and prove that they are worth what they want to get. If a woman has creative ability and wants to open a small shop, she could get into table linens. There is so much that can be done in linens today. But you have to work—it just doesn't happen. The linen shops around today are stagnant. I mean nothing exciting or commercial has been done with them.

I know that if I were to give up my shop, I would do table linens. I want to do a great deal in design. As for other women, it depends on their ability—their creative ability. What does a woman have the talent to do? Can she do flower arrangements? If she's good at it, she probably could go into business doing it for fancy money. Can she arrange to put on parties? I mean, planning the entire thing and dealing with guest lists and caterers? Then she could get into that.

There are a million and one things a woman can do.

Let's say a woman is extremely talented as a cook. She could open up a small restaurant—and I mean small. I've heard of a restaurant that just opened in New York that has only three tables. Naturally, it's such a chic thing to go to that you have to fight to get a reservation. And don't you think that in any large city in this country the woman who opens up the fanciest three-table restaurant in that city is going to clean up? Of course she is.

A woman can always earn money with her talent. Always. Most women have some kind of talent. Maybe it is dormant. Then, they've got to figure out what they are capable of doing and will enjoy doing. Success must be inevitable. Now you take a lot of these women who have started to put up certain things they're particularly good at. Like jellies, jams, that kind of thing. Their friends love these items and invariably if the woman wants to go commercial with the item she's going to do all right with it. Many businesses can be operated from the home. One woman I know used to do marvelous things with tea. She blended tea in her own home, using cloves, orange peel, herbs, and so forth.

All of her friends were constantly raving about her tea, so she decided to market it. Why, the thing is growing tremendously now. A few years ago a couple of young girls used to take ordinary green beans and pickle them in a certain way and use them for snacks with cocktails. I think they called their product Dilly Beans. They did very well with it.

Within the past couple of years people have become more aware that a bathroom has to be decorated—just like any other room in the house. And now, all of a sudden, bath shops are popping up all over the country. You can buy matching towel sets, fancy shower curtains, matching bath mats and any kind of accessory you want in these shops. They're booming. Here's a new field for somebody who has taste to get into. I can see a great need for shops that only supply items for individual rooms. Specializing is the secret. But, one word of caution—if you cannot build a better mousetrap, shy clear of starting your own business.

No matter what the business is, however, you've got to have a flair and originality. I'll give you a small example of what I mean. For years I wrote all my business letters in lower case. That is, I didn't use any capital letters in my correspondence. I used to get a lot of letters from customers commenting on the distinctive style. My letters are very personal and very informal. I write a letter the way I speak. I never use a salutation. I never use a closing such as "respectfully yours," or "sincerely yours." I wouldn't talk that way so why write a letter that way. It's very amusing at times. I start my letters by saying, "good morning, mrs. so-and-so."

I also am very advertising- and publicity-conscious. I usually write my own advertising copy. As for publicity, I'm very aware of that, too. About fifteen years ago, I let my press agent talk me into letting a bull into my shop. The rodeo was in town at Madison Square Garden, and the press agent said that he would like to see whether a bull behaved like a gentleman in a fine china shop. I was a little bit frightened about the whole thing because it could have been pretty cheap publicity. But, with tongue in cheek, I permitted him to go ahead with it.

Well, they brought down one of the bulls in the rodeo

and just managed to get it in through the double doors
of the shop. We had cleared an aisle about halfway down
the store. The television cameras were there, and the news-
papers, and the radio. There was one hell of a crowd of
people. Anyhow, they brought this beast in the store and
I went back to my office. I wouldn't go near the thing.
I didn't know what was going to happen. The bull was
surprisingly very docile and walked very gently. But he
was being a little too docile. So they gave him a little prod,
and kept walking him up and down the aisle, which was
pretty narrow, and then they put him in front of a beautiful table setting. The bull looked it over and then stuck
out his tongue and licked the table decoration. And down
the damned thing went. That night on the Camel's news
program, the film of that bull's tongue in slow motion as it
licked the table decoration was simply fantastic. The
announcer was fabulous, too. It was great. Just great publicity.

But not everything goes smoothly. It takes a lot to
make a million dollars, I'll tell you that. I can lose it faster.
About three years ago I got involved with a gadget called
Puncherino. Puncherino is an inflated ball attached by a
rubber band to a pair of goggles. The idea is you're supposed to put the goggles on and then sock away at the ball
to develop your co-ordination and skill. As far as an adult
is concerned, it is a great tranquilizer. I used to put it on
three or four times a day and belt it around just to release
energy. It has play value for the children and they love it.

Anyhow, I saw this thing in Italy where it was made by
a man in his home. I set up a little factory in Italy to manufacture the product and I thought I'd just bring it into
this country and in two or three months time make a very

fast bundle on it. It was right after the Hula-Hoop craze and I thought I'd cash in on something that was even better. Boy, was I wrong.

I didn't know much about the toy business. I didn't realize that you had to spend a fortune on television. I didn't know that retailers wouldn't buy the thing unless you did TV promotion. And this is not peanuts. This runs into a lot of money.

I've learned a valuable lesson from this experience. One should never spread himself too thin. You should take one marketing area at a time, absorb that area, and then go to another area. When the TV promotion went on I didn't have the merchandise placed in the stores. It was one hell of a mess, but I still believe it's a great item. I don't call Puncherino a failure. The item is good; it was only because of my inexperience and lack of time that it did not become the successor to the Hula-Hoop and a financial bonanza.

This experience proves out the old adage, "Shoemaker, stick to your last."

You can't learn good taste from books, or from school. You've either got to be born with it or to acquire it slowly over the years. My taste is just something inherent. I think that a person has to be surrounded by lovely things and this is how they develop an appreciation of good taste. Now people will say that in certain areas of the country there are different standards of taste. This premise is absolutely false. We have customers from all over and I have found that good taste is appreciated by people everywhere. Granted, the way of living may be more informal in one area than another. But good taste is good taste.

I have never had any qualms in introducing new ideas

or color schemes. For instance, many years ago, gold was associated with being ostentatious but today it is quite a different thing. I have been a firm advocate of the use of gold appointments for a long, long time. We have a lot of future brides who come in and want sterling flatwear and when we suggest gold they shy away from it until they've seen it Carolated with china. It's always a great satisfaction to me when we convince a young couple that they should have gold instead of sterling silver. It's almost like a religious conversion and you know when you convert someone you get pleasure out of that. I recently had a couple in and when I mentioned gold they said it was out of the question. But I set up a table with china and glass and then I put on the silver flatware. Then I replaced the silver with gold flatware and the transformation was fantastic. They immediately called their parents and told them that they had decided on gold.

It is the satisfaction of situations such as this that prompts me to say that I don't think I'll ever retire. I couldn't be happy retired. I think I would stagnate if I had nothing to do. I couldn't stand that. The only thing that could ever force me out of business is my old nemesis, lack of help. Many years ago I had a young girl who started with me as a maid at eight dollars a week. She ended up making a hundred and fifty a week as my top assistant, but that girl had talent to her fingertips. She was my right arm and instinctively knew that this item went with that item. She never had to be told. She almost breathed the way I did. Unfortunately, she died two years ago. And to get a girl like that today, I would pay two hundred and fifty dollars a week, but I can't find anybody like that. And she started as a maid.

Let me tell you one last story. Ten years ago a young man walked in and said, "Miss Stupell, I want to work for you." He had a Ph.D. and came in right off the street. I liked him. I said, "How much do you want?" He said, "Well, I just want to learn." He started at fifty-five dollars a week. I had no job but I gave him one in unit control. He was there two weeks and I promoted him to an assistant's job. In one month he became my assistant. In six months he was running my desk. He was great, just fabulous. He left after several years to start his own advertising firm, which is very successful.

I don't have any Ph.D.'s walking in here any more. This younger generation doesn't seem to have any ambition. How much can I get? What are the hours? Is there overtime? That's all they're interested in. In short, their philosophy is that the world owes them a living. This is a real problem. I worry about it quite a bit.

V

Philip J. Sagona is thirty-one years old and owns Lancôme Perfumes (U.S.). He was born in Brooklyn and his first job consisted of supervising a shoeshine stand operation. According to one of his many press agents, he is able to raise eighty million dollars on the strength of his signature, which, in terms of American businessmen, makes his a fairly potent signature indeed.

PHILIP J. SAGONA

My first job, when I was eight years old, was running a shoeshine stand. The only trouble was there were four corners on the street intersection that I wanted to work on. Supposedly everyone hung out there and got their shoes shined. Now, when I wanted to shine shoes there weren't any corners left so I had to derive means of getting a corner. So I built a shoestand and I had four kids working for me—the four kids who normally worked the four corners of the intersection. I was a supervisor, so actually I never became a shoeshine boy in the true sense of the word.

To capture these four corners I had to sell the idea to each of these boys to work for me and under certain circumstances. They all thought that I was being unfair by taking their corners over. My way of going about it was to sell one boy and then he sold the others. And my way of selling him was to give him a portion of what I would get, but the others never knew it. So I never really sold the other three. I had him sell the other three, so, actually, I was always selling. Now that kid that I sold on this concept got twenty-five per cent of the profits that I got. And I had to pay a storekeeper thirty dollars that I had borrowed from him to build the booth. On an average weekend, I could make myself about fifteen dollars, which was a lot of money then. I gave the money to my mother. That shoestand still stands in Brooklyn today.

I was born in Brooklyn, New York, on March the third, 1933. At the age of about seven, we moved from the Bay Ridge section of Brooklyn, to Williamsburg, Brooklyn. At the age of about twelve, I had to support myself and my mother. Williamsburg is a very poor neighborhood, a neighborhood where it's congested, a neighborhood where people live in railroad flats. It's even difficult to describe how people actually live in such a modern society today and the fact that this kind of living still goes on. As a very young boy I dreamed of the day when I could move from such a neighborhood and environment.

Like many young boys, I guess I always dreamed of the financial environment I wanted to have around me as I grew up. I never had much. For example, the average child has a bicycle. I didn't. The average child can run to the ice cream wagon when it comes around the block and I couldn't. And it became extremely frustrating. You have no idea. You cannot describe the deeply annoying feeling that comes from being born to a certain class and then having no jurisdictional power to overcome this. And the only way to overcome this is by your own aggressiveness—through the effort and force of your own will power, which enables you to progress and gain the financial means to get the things you want.

I was always a bad loser. I hated to lose and even now I hate to lose. I like to think I'm always a winner, which was why I did many things with greater practice than the average person, like basketball. I couldn't stand to lose. I was a sore loser and I made sure I never lost.

At the age of thirteen, I was able to get an athletic scholarship for basketball to high school. I achieved this by thinking of it as a goal, a goal which I set out to achieve at the age of eight, nine, ten, eleven, and twelve years of age. I was outstanding as an athlete, although it was a God-given ability. But nothing is given, and I would practice and practice and practice my athletic abilities to make sure I was always the so-called outstanding player, hoping to become a star.

I chose to go to St. John's Preparatory School in Brooklyn, which gave me the scholarship. It is one of the outstanding prep schools in the East, and my full tuition was paid. During those years of high school I still was a sorehead and hated to lose, although when I did lose people never knew it. It just used to eat within me. I never took it out on people like some will and be an outward sorehead. I always would take it out on myself. When I lost or did not get my way, I used to constantly relive the situation to find out why I didn't play well, or what went wrong. Why did we lose? I would ask myself. I just couldn't stand it. I couldn't stand the thought of losing.

This drive of mine no doubt came about because of the environment in which I lived. I never was spoiled in the sense that I never had a family to give me the things that I wanted. I had to achieve my own goals and what started my mind thinking that it wasn't success which I wanted in life, which to me means money and dollars, but it was always trying to achieve a goal. I wanted to be recognized and I felt that as a young boy the greatest sin I could commit was not take the true potential out of myself. Of all the sins I could ever dream about I believed the greatest sin a man could commit is never to reach his full potential in life. And I realized this as a young boy, that I was sinning by not giving my true abilities and by being unfulfilled.

Success—and money—were not the important things to me. I wanted to have an achievement. I wanted to be the outstanding athlete, to have the highest marks. I wanted to achieve the goal of being a college graduate because in the neighborhood I came from there was no such thing as anyone even attending college, never mind graduating. I wanted to graduate with recognition. There wasn't any envy in the neighborhood. Actually, there was a great deal of respect. The other kids wondered, how could this one person do everything that I was doing? Go to school, play ball, work every night until two in the morning. Well, how does one do this? Through sheer sacrifice. I sacrificed a great many things, whereas the others did not. A lot of people talk ambition, but they're not really ambitious.

I have always hated to lose at anything, and I still do.

I don't believe in detouring around competition. I like to hit it head-on. Nobody has a monopoly on brain power.

There's no secret about the success I have achieved. I don't make snap judgments. I plan carefully and then do what I have planned. I weigh in advance possibilities of success or failure.

Often success is the result of meeting the right people at the right time and the right place. It's also a matter of seizing every opportunity. Lots of people say you must have luck to get ahead, but I don't agree. I make my own luck by planning and by working hard.

Beauty products are big business. It's a four-hundred-million-dollar-a-year industry and a highly competitive one. To succeed requires a great sales ability. It also requires imagination, creativity, a knowledge of merchandising techniques and good quality in products.

Most important of all is a knowledge of finance, of costs. That's vital in any business today. I study my cost figures because they tell me what direction I should take.

My second job, when I was about twelve years old, was to clean up St. Joseph's Patron Church after the bingo game. Bingo ended at midnight and I would go down and clean up. I was only a child at the time and I went to the parish one night and asked a priest if I could have the job of cleaning up. He sent me to the superintendent and he said, "No, you're just a kid." I was very annoyed at losing out on this so I looked in one night to see what the professional men did when they cleaned up. It was very easy. They turned the tables over, unscrewed the legs and carried the tables off and then swept up the floors. They were getting paid a good sum of money, so I went to the priest and told him, "Suppose I told you a way of cleaning up this place in the same amount of time which would cost you about a quarter of what you're paying?" He said, "If you can show me how to do that, you can have the job." I brought in eight kids and we did the job and we got paid a quarter of what the professional janitors were getting. Here again I had these kids working for me. I became a so-called supervisor.

When I was twenty-two years old, a man named Revson literally changed my life. I had finished St. John's University on an athletic scholarship, one of twenty-two offered to me, and was selling Royal typewriters in the garment center. I was my usual frustrated self: trying to get ahead and knowing and realizing that at my age selling typewriters was not for me.

One night I was sitting in the living room watching the "$64,000 Question," which was the rage of the nation if you recall. I said to my mother, "This is the kind of company I should be with. I should be in the cosmetic industry. I like this kind of thing, I understand fashion, I understand color. This is a very fascinating company. I'd love to get into this kind of business, and I think I'll apply for a job tomorrow."

I found out through my contacts who owned Revlon. He was Charles Revson. I tried to reach him at home. He wasn't home for three days. The man was busy all the time, but I felt that I would rather wait than make the mistake of applying cold as a salesman. I had gone into drugstores and department stores to see what it was all about, and it was absolutely fascinating. I love women. I just adore them. I love to be in their company and anything to do with women made it more fascinating for me. Finally, I got Mr. Charles, as he is called, at home one night. "Mr. Revson," I said, "this is Philip Sagona." I was very dramatic. "I've been watching your program the '$64,000 Question,'" I said, "and I find it very stimulating." "Thank you," he said. Then I said, "I'd like to work for you." At this point he said, "Is that why you're calling me?" "Yes," I said, "I'm one of the most outstanding salesmen in the garment center and I'd like to work for your company. I know I could do well." He said, "Well, you must be crazy." Then he said, "Why don't you go to my personnel department and fill out an application?" "Oh no," I said, "I'm not just the run of the mill. I'm out to get this job. I just don't want to be pushed aside." He said, "You go in to see Mr. So-and-So. I'll tell him you'll be calling."

So I went in and was interviewed. And of course with Mr. Revson giving me the lead, the red carpet was put out for me. They said, "Keep a close eye on this fellow, because when Mr. Revson recommends someone to the sales department, he must be someone." They gave me an aptitude test and I was hired at about four hundred dollars a month, plus a company car, bonus and then commission over sales. At the time that was a handsome salary. I was hired as a drugstore salesman and the territory they gave me was the Bronx. It was a very difficult territory. I felt that the selling was very easy as compared to selling a product which is not consumed. A door-to-door product was always more difficult. It was inevitable that each time I walked into a store, I would get an order for Revlon, but the whole idea was to get the order to be twice its normal size and then merchandise it.

I worked at Revlon as a salesman, an account executive, a district sales manager, making me the youngest sales manager in the history of the company. I was there for about three and a half years and I left Revlon for nothing more than financial reasons. I then went to Chanel and I only stayed there a very short time, seven months. It was not the type of firm I liked, in the sense that it was not as promotional-minded and it didn't fit my character and personality. Then I had an opportunity to go to work for Lanvin, and I stayed there for about three years. During that period of time I became the director of marketing.

The last two years at Lanvin I had the desire to get into my own business. Because, during this time, I had been investing my handsome salary in the stock market. Stocks were doing very well, as you know, and the market was at a booming peak. I didn't just play around. I would not advise any young person to gamble, because one who is young doesn't have enough money to gamble. But, since your money only makes four per cent or so interest at the bank, I see no reason why you cannot buy five shares of this and ten shares of that. It's a very intelligent thing to do. You can start with five hundred or a thousand dollars. That is how I started. That is how Bernard Baruch started. All the rich were once poor, and they had to start somewhere, and I recommend very much that the young fellows learn about the stock market.

Also, because of my contacts, I was able to help two or three corporations merge, and from these deals I made what is called a finder's fee. In a relatively short period of time, I had what amounted to a great sum of money. Without going into details, I will say that Dun and Bradstreet has me rated. To buy Lancôme it took a good sum of money and then I borrowed the rest of the money. You see, when you have that kind of cash, you can get loans against your money.

Lancôme is one of the prestige and exclusive fragrance houses in the United States, and their products are sold only in the specialty shops, such as Bergdorf-Goodman, Saks Fifth Avenue, Bonwit Teller, Lord and Taylor, and stores of that type. It took me two years to find the company. I did a lot of looking around. I went out and spoke to a lot of corporations and a lot of corporations were willing to sell. But they were asking prices that were a million or two million dollars more than what they were really worth.

Going to the bank to borrow money is one of the greatest things that ever happened to me. It didn't happen soon enough. You walk into a bank and tell the banker you want to make a loan. And then the bankers says, "Well, what do you want to make the loan for?" And then the banks give it a tremendous amount of research. The banks just don't give you the loan. What they put you through is worse than the F.B.I. It's incredible, it's unbelievable.

In our company, we have one very famous fragrance, Magie, and this does the greatest portion of our volume. It is a very beautiful, sensual, sophisticated, elegant fragrance, and what has helped it a great deal is the fact that Jacqueline Kennedy uses it.

I've now had Lancôme for more than two years and in this time we've doubled our volume. In order to get this volume to double as we did, you must give the consumers that which they want, and we developed thirteen new products. We designed and manufactured aerosol sprays for perfume and toilet water. We developed new lipsticks, new eye products, new eye makeup. We had to regenerate and revitalize the corporation to do this. We have a prestige operation.

I am sure that I am not unlike other executives in that the first thing I do when I get to my desk in the morning is to say a prayer. I say a prayer that everything I do and all the decisions that I make will be correct for this day. I don't think this is being sacrilegious at all. All I am asking is that He guide me to make the right decisions. When one goes into battle he says a prayer asking that he come out alive. This is the same thing. I am going to battle. In business you are really shooting and you are really getting shot at by the enemy all day long. And I am just making a short prayer that will help me make the right decisions because my decisions affect a lot of people. I ask that my decisions, which I will make, will not in any way hurt or hamper the future of the company.

It's amazing how many decisions you make. Maybe in the course of a day you will have to make forty to fifty decisions, because that is what your job is as an executive. During one day there are at least five major decisions which inevitably involve ten, twenty or thirty thousand dollars. You must be careful! Your decisions are affecting the lives of the people you hire and fire, and the responsibility is great.

When you hire a sales manager, as I have, who is twenty-eight years old, you are not only hiring him but you are hiring his family. He has four children, and my decision to hire him and my decision to do the right thing about him affects his whole life. When he leaves work at six o'clock his happiness at work affects his whole future at home. If the man is unhappy at work, then eventually his wife is unhappy. Before you know it, the wife begins to dislike the boss.

When one is forced to do something, he becomes an imprisoned man. And to be forced to be poor is a terrible thing. But when you have the freedom and the democracy that our country offers, why, the future belongs to us and you just go out and take it. And the future costs nothing. I didn't do anything unusual because it doesn't cost anything. Our freedom is here. Nothing stopped me from turning around and getting a good education.

There is no exact science to success. The man who says that success is an exact science and you can put it on a slide rule or measure it with calipers is wrong. If they could measure it, they'd be billionaires. But I do feel that there is a science to achievement, but not success.

To achieve a goal, you cannot be a hypocrite. You can only bluff so much. Eventually, it catches up with you. There are guys who literally bluff almost their whole way through life. They bluff and bluff but eventually they are caught and are recognized. I know executives, literally, who have bluffed their way into management and high, important levels. You can bluff through personality and politicking. Some fellows will bluff and bluff and bluff and eventually they are recognized. There are a lot of executives who are bluffing at their jobs and are paid thirty-five thousand dollars a year.

The first basic value of life that I have is to respect myself and give myself what I am entitled to. This is self-preservation. Another of my basic values is to serve God and therefore serve myself because this gives me peace of mind. I must have peace of mind. Without your peace of mind, you have nothing. And don't let anybody kid you. You can only have peace of mind when you have peace of mind with God.

You cannot have peace of mind with money, or friendship, or travel. These never give peace of mind because, unfortunately, your mind is always with you. So this is the first thing, the first problem that you must remedy. You must have peace of mind with God.

Another of my values is to get along and associate with people because this is the second most important thing in life. The third of my values is to live a life with another person. A man must take a wife because we are always looking for the other half of our lives and we cannot be happy alone. We must have a partner. So these are three very important points: We must love and serve God and thus achieve self-preservation through God; we must get along with and serve and honor our friends; and, thirdly, no one can live alone and you must have a spouse to bring you true happiness.

I never get lonely. Sometimes I get depressed when I see that people will not accept a person like myself, without even taking time to find out about me. You know, I am a target right now. I'm right at the top and everyone is trying to shoot me off the top. I'm a sitting duck up there and they're all trying to shoot me down. People and even companies are trying this and it's a terrible thing because one of the greatest sins in life is envy. It's nothing new to me because as an athlete I often recognized it. I have nothing against it. If anything, I pity these people.

But I am very disappointed in certain people, certain

friends, whom I thought were friends. Call it envy, call it jealousy. It's so petty I don't like to talk about it. I want to be above it. I don't have time to talk about this nonsense.

I get up very early every day, usually about six-thirty. I have breakfast with my mother and that is the only time I see her, usually. I am in the office early and I am on the telephone immediately. I usually go to my private club for dinner, and attend a lot of fashionable cocktail parties that I am invited to during the course of a week. The average day is very hectic and with a lot of catastrophes and personnel problems.

I have a good temper, though, and I feel that I have respect for the organization and my people and thus they respect me. To me, the field of perfume and cosmetics is the most fascinating business in the world and I love it. It is a part of show business. It's the most fascinating business in the world because it all has to do with women, and what could be more exciting than women? The industry is becoming more and more an important part of big industry. I would recommend young men wholeheartedly to go into it. It is a field which hasn't been scratched. It has just begun. It is a field where young men are needed because most perfume-cosmetic companies are run by a lot of older-type people. Young men are desperately needed, young men with college educations who want to get into sales, merchandising, marketing, advertising, and promotion. The field is wide open and corporations in our industry are looking and constantly interviewing people.

Aside from love, of course, the most romantic subject in the world, to me, to talk about is perfume. It means romance, emotion, love, sexuality, sensuality. Perfume is the most impressionable thing that affects a man because your nose thinks faster than your mind. You could smell perfume tonight and no matter where you are, five years later, if you smell the same perfume again, you would think of the woman who wore it five years previously. You know, if men wore perfume they would make better lovers because the sense of smell is the most stimulating of all senses.

It is true that I have had luck, but I have made my luck. I don't wish to be a dramatic, egotistical person, but I am where I am because I wanted to be where I am and if young people would only take this attitude and earnestly desire and want these certain things, they would achieve them. If they keep going through life halfheartedly praying for certain goals, they will never achieve them. They must earnestly want to achieve a goal. People must know where they want to go and what they wish to do. But people do not wish to go to night school. They are very selfish and they don't want to give up their time. I could talk for hours on this subject because I want to put it across to young people. If the older people haven't achieved success at their age, they are never going to make it.

My only problem is that I do not have enough time in my day to do the things I want to do to accomplish the additional goals I have. But what I am trying to do is to hire people to help me. I am surrounding myself with bright and intelligent men and women so they can run things for me and I can keep projecting. I don't believe in doing details. I want to put my feet up on the desk and think and plan how to accomplish greater goals. I am not paid to do the detail work. I hire intelligent people to do the details. I delegate, organize and then plan ahead.

I think our government should take the time to emphasize to the younger people how important it is to achieve the true potential in themselves in school. If the school systems were able to get the student to take the true potential out of himself, then we would have an ample supply of qualified and intelligent students. But instead everything is becoming robotlike. Everything is tests, and more tests. If anything, tests aren't any good. If I got a ninety on a test and you got one hundred this doesn't mean that you are ten per cent better in brainpower. What tests don't measure is the will to do.

It is those who have the will to do who progress. The teachers in the schools must teach the students how to have the will to accomplish because this is what the Russians are doing. And the Russian students *do* have the will —they have the will to get ahead, to capture, to conquer the world.

One must believe in himself, and to be happy with one's self, you must believe in something. No man is an island, no matter how big a man you are. And the greatest man who ever walked on the face of the earth had twelve people helping him. If a man thinks he can go through life without people helping him, he is not intelligent. I don't like to cry sour grapes about the fact that I was a poor boy and, you know, it is very difficult to talk about it. I can get very steamed up in talking about success. It's just that it is difficult to put the ideas across because words are dead unless they're spoken.

But my success has come through myself. Most people

dream of success by means of wishing and this just doesn't happen. Because when you walk up Fifth Avenue you can look up at this cement jungle we live in. These buildings have opportunities in them, and the opportunities are unlimited. There are corporations looking for people and the young guys and girls are America. It's all for them, take it, it costs nothing.

VI

Martin Ransohoff represents the new breed in Hollywood—the independent producer who doesn't own a studio. Ransohoff, chairman of the board and majority stockholder of Filmways, Inc., began his career making commercials for television and eventually moved into television and movie production.

MARTIN RANSOHOFF

I was born in New Orleans in 1927. My father is a coffee importer. I led a reasonably normal upper middle-class life. There was no Horatio Alger stuff. I'd like to be able to say that when I was four years old Dad took me down to the mines and I put a hat on, grabbed a pick and worked my way through kindergarten. But I can't say it. No such dramatic nonsense involved.

When I was very young I had a fascination for the movies, which was compulsive at the very least. I think that my family thought it was more neurotic tendency than compulsiveness. And there's a very thin line between compulsive behavior and neurotic behavior. My family had moved to Connecticut when I was young. Occasionally, my parents used to bring the three kids—my brother, my sister, and myself—into New York City from time to time and we'd come in to see exhibitions at the Museum of Modern Art and the Museum of Natural History. The kids and my parents would be playing games like Ghost and Pool in the car to pass the time and I would be involved in looking at the movie signs.

We'd be driving through Times Square and my father would say, "Look at the Camel sign where the smoke is coming out." And I would say, "Look at the Criterion." I was fascinated with the movies from the time I could go and enjoy them. I used to get a tremendous kick and thrill out of going to pictures. I still like them a hell of a lot, by the way. Saturdays were terrific. I'd go and watch the serials—the guy jumping off the top of the railroad, the girl leaping off the horse, the whole scan. For example, Errol Flynn was my idol when I was a kid. "Robin Hood," "Dawn Patrol," "Captain Blood"—I used to love all those adventure epics. I used to love to see those pictures. Good pictures. It wasn't a matter of going for junk. It was just anything that was good. I still vividly remember pictures like "Men With Wings" with Fred MacMurray. I don't think anybody could have come from a less theatrical family than I did. My parents, who had never been movie-goers, would see Fred Astaire and Ginger Rogers once in a while. My brother and sister were never much for going to movies. They saw "Snow White" once, but I probably saw it four or five times.

In 1945, I went to college—Colgate. Right after the war,

with so many G.I.'s demanding to get in school, Colgate was one of those that thought my grades were good enough to get in. I feel that college has very little bearing on a man's career in terms of what you learn being applicable to the kind of career you have later on. It can give you a certain background in the arts and background in terms of reading and a small amount of the fundamentals, but that's about it. For instance, the economics you learn in college hardly prepare you for the business world. If you want to become an accountant then the college business courses are O.K. But the rules of buy and sell which run most businesses are learned on the road. Nobody can teach you these rules out of a book. Very few people will acknowledge that college itself provided any basic fundamentals in terms of business acumen. What it does is provide you with a certain base for reading which you wouldn't do otherwise. It gives you a well-rounded background and a chance to do some reflective thinking under conditions that don't prevail otherwise.

One thing did happen to me at Colgate that probably had more effect on me from a commercial standpoint than anything else. During the summer of my sophomore year, I was kind of hard-pressed for cash, between my automobile and social activities. I couldn't get my father too much interested in my problem and realizing that I was running kind of short of money I figured I'd better go out and make some dough. I had heard fantastic stories from one of my fraternity brothers that you could make seventy dollars a day selling that expensive kitchenware door to door. I figured I had better take a crack at it, so when the fellow from Alcoa came around recruiting I went, got interviewed, and signed up. At first, I was horrified at the incredible problem of opening a door cold and standing there with a book in your hand having the expression of guilt that one wears at first when selling door to door. I think the door-to-door salesman is marked by his apathy or his look of guilt or a combination of the two.

Think of it. You have to push your way through the door and get in to sell a basically hostile housewife something that costs twice as much as an item that could be purchased in a store. I took the job and was successful at it and the experience was without question the best experience I've ever had in my life in preparing me for the jungle after college. I not only worked in the summer but part time through the school year. When things would get fiscally tough at Colgate, I'd go into the hills with my little package of tin and push these one hundred twenty-five dollar cooking-equipment specials. The commissions were in the neighborhood of forty per cent of the gross sale. If you sold a hundred-dollar unit you'd get forty bucks, which in college was a small fortune—at least a couple of weeks' pocket money.

I think that the grounding and the schooling that somebody gets from door-to-door contact is fantastic. There's no way to evaluate how valuable it is. To me, at the age of twenty-three or twenty-four, I was a cold practitioner of the psychology of selling which, broken down, is simply: the allies overcoming the enemy. The tools that you need to break down resistance—I learned all that selling pots and pans. And to know when to close. The important thing in selling is to know when to close a deal. And the difference between those that really make it and those who don't make it is the one who closes. A closer is the one who knows the exact moment when a deal works. He's not a moment too soon or a moment too late. You go through eight or nine hundred closings on pots and pans and by God you get a tremendous instinct of feeling for the moment. Timing. Timing is a tremendous thing in business and in the entertainment business it's almost everything.

When I got out of college my dream, like all good boys from Darien, New Canaan, Greenwich, Montclair, Great Neck, and so on, was to work in advertising. It was the "in" thing to do and I was sucked up in it. So I went to Young and Rubicam and I was told by the top brass there that I had to go into the mail room for a couple of months, like everybody else, and not to worry because I'd be on my way after that formality was over.

When my shoe leather wore out I pointed out to them that I wasn't living off my father and that fifty bucks a week was not even taking care of the cleaning bills and shoe leather. I got moved into the marketing department where I could have the privilege and thrill of checking Schlitz bottles on Broadway. I was young and decided that there must be another route because I thought that I had more talent than sitting around counting Schlitz bottles after I had put in my apprenticeship in the shoe leather department. So I left.

I sold Mexican pumpkin seeds for a few months and then worked for a textile company for another few months. Finally I decided to go to Europe, just getting away from everything to decide what the hell I wanted to do with myself. I needed some quick money to get there so I made a deal with a Ford dealer in Connecticut. I would go up into the hills and buy used cars and bring them down and we'd clean them up and run them out. I picked up three or four thousand dollars in three months doing this and then I packed a bag, jumped on a freighter and went to Europe. I stayed over there for six months.

While I was over there I did a hell of a lot of thinking. I knew instinctively that I was falling into the classical rut of the jerk from Suburbia. He goes to college, gets out, does what everyone else does, and plugs and slugs along. I just felt that there must be more to life than this, you know? I knew that I didn't want to be another sheep on the train back and forth to Connecticut with the picket fence, the station wagon, the kids, the coronary, the whole bit with insuring yourself for three hundred thousand dollars so the premium is so much you can't take a vacation in the summer. I just didn't want to become a Babbitt— the guy in the Cadillac with the button-down shirt, the gray flannel slacks, the brown scuffies with the little Argyle socks. I knew this was what I didn't want.

The way I figured it was, it wasn't a question of rising to the vice-presidency of Chrysler. I figured that would happen, but how do you make a living and avoid becoming a vice-president at Chrysler? And I wanted material things, too. I'm not a guy in a torn sweatshirt living in the Village. So I had the confusion that you always have at that age when you just don't know what to do with yourself.

When I got back from Europe I decided that somehow I was going to stay in the creative area—hopefully, television, broadcasting, motion pictures. There I was, off the boat, I had a girl I wanted to marry, and I was in debt to the tune of eight hundred dollars and I had to tap my father for about sixty bucks for walking-around money. And I'm staggering around New York with the Colgate College placement bureau sending me those little post cards which say, "There is an opportunity at Vicks Chemical. . . ." I said to myself, Oh no, no nasal-drop signs in the stores for me, no G.E. training program, none of that for me. To show you how really incredibly frank and circumstantial life is, I met a guy I knew at Y. and R. and he said, "What's up, kid?" I said, "Nothing." Well, this guy said, "I just came from a screening and I saw a one-minute film that we just did for a baby-food sponsor. The room is filled with guys smoking cigars and they all look like Hollywood castoffs. And the film cost three thousand dollars." "Three thousand dollars?" I said. "Yeah," he said, "and you know there's got to be some jack rubbing off somewhere in three thousand dollars for a one-minute film."

Now this was in 1951 and television was just getting started. So this fellow from Y. and R. suggested that I get into the making of commercials. We got out the telephone book to look up the names of film companies and I spotted one named Caravel Films. I went over to their offices, saw the president of the firm, told him I wanted a job selling film and I said that I had some experience. He hired me on the spot for a hundred-dollar-a-week draw against commission.

The long and the short of it is I did around a quarter of a million dollars of business the first year that I worked for this outfit.

The job was good for me. During this period I spent a lot of time in the cutting room. I did some writing. I even got in a little directing. And I realized that I had a real feeling for the whole field of visual presentation. I felt for the first time in my life that, O.K., this is it. Somehow, I knew that this was it. We had a disagreement over commissions owed me and I quit after fifteen months.

So, I was out on the street again. Then I heard about a guy over on the West Side of New York with a small film business, who was looking for a partner. His name was Ed Kaspar and he made an industrial film every now and then and he had a small color laboratory. I set up a meeting with Kaspar and we decided to form a company. We capitalized it for two hundred dollars and called the outfit Filmways. He had one hundred shares of stock, and so did I. We found office space over a packing plant on West Fifty-seventh Street between Ninth and Tenth Avenues. It was one room and it was the smallest thing you ever saw. This was the company. The idea was that Kaspar would be the technical man and I would be the outside and selling man. The only thing we had going for us was that when we formed the company in 1952 we were on the absolute ground floor of television.

So I figured, well, I've got to get this thing off the ground somehow, so I came up with a plan for doing experimental test films and I got the Colgate Company interested. The idea was to develop a way to pre-test commercials using an inexpensive, sixteen millimeter method of production. This gave the advertiser a chance to pre-test his commercial and also a chance to see what the full-scale commercial would look like—all at a reasonable cost. I needed a gimmick. We had to have some way of getting a crack at the big commercial contracts, or we had nothing. I thought that this would do it. There we were, a brand-new company, terrible facilities in a horrible part of town, and we had to get exposure. Even though we were working out of a hole in the wall, I had to get something going.

Once we got started, I had a lot of contacts and I thought we could work our way in, getting test films to do, and then move on to the sponsors and the advertising agencies. Well, our first year we did roughly one hundred thirty thousand dollars' worth of business. This may sound like a lot, but it isn't. But the thing is, we did it with nothing. We did it with mirrors. No equipment, that little room we called a studio, it was a miracle we did that much business. The second year we did about four hundred seventy thousand dollars; the third year we did more than eight hundred thousand, and then all of a sudden we were on our way. The fourth year we did about a million two, the fifth year, 1957, almost two million, and in 1958, more than three million. And the company just kept building.

Now don't forget, this was an embryonic business. And we weren't unique. There must have been two hundred little companies like ours operating in New York at the time. They were all over the city, operating out of telephone booths. Most of them folded. We flourished, and I don't exactly know why, except we worked hard as hell and probably because we were better than most of the guys in it. There were a lot of clowns in the business, too. That didn't hurt us. We must have netted around seventeen grand that first year. The next year we split about thirty, and by the time we went public in 1958 we netted around two hundred twenty-eight thousand dollars after taxes.

Originally, the theory was that I did the producing and the contact and the creative work, and Kaspar would do the directing, the stage work, and the mechanics. But as the company grew and grew and the organization started to form, his area remained pretty confined and mine got, well, it got nightmarish. I was shouldering a tremendously large portion of the operation, and he felt he was working too hard. At one point it became, "Either you buy me out or I'll buy you out."

So I bought him out. Then I had to recapitalize the company, and by the time that little complicated mess was completed I wound up with about sixty-five per cent of the company. We then completely recapitalized the company and went public late in 1957. We sold a hundred and fifty thousand shares to the public for just under five dollars a share. It's moved a lot since then.

The following year the company grew and flourished at a greater pace because I was able to take other people into the company. It became a much more fluid operation. We began getting into television commercial production in a very big way. We had done a job for the Ford Motor Company through the J. Walter Thompson Agency for a million dollars. It was an entire advertising campaign called "Around the World in '58 Fords." Then, because of the foreign experience we had had in dealing with Ford, we got a lot of foreign commercial work for other advertisers—Procter and Gamble, Noxema, more stuff for Ford. We began to do a lot of work in Europe. We became the company that got involved overseas and that was capable of handling an overseas assignment.

I had no doubts at all about the success of the company.

It was just hammer and nails and there were never any questions in my mind about our direction once I started to see the light of day. Back around '58, I made up my mind that the company should expand and diversify if it was really going to make any money. I thought that the commercial business was very limited and was going to be less and less lucrative. I felt that in order to really make the company move, we had to get into television programming and movie production. I felt that I had the ability to make things go in that direction. I was getting mixed up with a lot of things and had started doing some subcontract work for major companies.

We then took on the technical production of the Winston Churchill series for ABC, which was our first television production that was non-commercial. About the same time, George Burns's production company on the West Coast was being dissolved, so I hired Al Simon, who had been Burns's production head, to become head of our television production. One of the things we inherited was "21 Beacon Street," which had been designed by Simon as a summer replacement show. It was a brainy detective show. I made arrangements to do the financing and boom, we were in the television business.

Al Simon was also instrumental in what really put us on the television map, "Mr. Ed," the talking horse. Al had a pilot on the show and it hadn't moved. So, I sold it to Studebaker and they in turn sponsored the show on local stations around the country. The thing became a big hit on television. For the first time, a syndicated show went network and it helped put Filmways and our TV operation in a strong position.

Then things started to happen fast and we started buying ideas and developing projects. In the meantime, we had been trying to get Paul Henning back into television. He is the guy who had the idea for the "Beverly Hillbillies." You see, my theory of the whole business is based on creative talent. Equipment, facilities don't mean a thing. It's the guy who can come up with an idea and execute it well. Henning is a brilliant writer and a wonderful guy. We had lunch and Paul said he might be interested in coming back to television if the proper idea, the proper show concept, came along. I asked him to develop a rural show. I felt a rural comedy had a chance at this time. There's always been a limitless market for rural stuff, like "Grand Ole Opry."

Paul came back a week later and said, "I have a hell of an idea. I will take an Ozark family and let a big oil company come in and discover oil under a little chicken patch in their back yard. This family will be so far back in the hills that they never have even seen a television set. They get paid twenty-five million dollars by an oil company because this is one of the richest pools of oil ever discovered. And we'll have a daughter in the family, Ellie May, who is past the age of eligibility in the hills—she's seventeen. So the family decides to move to civilization to give Ellie May another chance at life and they move to Beverly Hills."

That's all I needed to hear. I met with his lawyer that afternoon and committed us to one hundred thousand dollars for the making of the pilot. I gave Paul complete creative control. Now, there was a question of protecting the hundred thousand. Let me tell you about the business end of the television game. You're much better off having a network as a partner. There aren't many half-hours and hours open. If you make a deal with a network, you more readily secure an outlet for your show. All the pilots in the world don't do you a bit of good unless they're on the air. So, we went into partnership with CBS on the show. They reimbursed us for the hundred thousand dollars and they now own half of the show.

Actually, it's not that easy. After you make the split with the network then you start giving points—percentage points—away. There are tremendous payments to be made —to Henning, to other creative talent. We ended up owning forty-two and a half per cent of the show. If you're lucky with a network show, you hope to get your costs out on your two- or three-year network run. If you can do this, you consider you're doing well. Then, you have income coming in from merchandising and other subsidiary sources. If the show is very successful, this auxiliary income becomes very important during the third, fourth, and fifth year of the run. Now, if the show is a smash, like "Hillbillies," then your potential future syndication values of it can be phenomenal.

It was a great idea. It had identifiable characters that are sympathetic and in whom the audience can have a rooting interest. Then there's the glitter and gloss of Beverly Hills, the snobbery. You have wonderful comedic opportunities in the contrast between the grass roots of this family and the snobs in Beverly Hills.

It was really a sensational idea. If some young man had walked into our offices off the street with the same idea we'd have taken it and developed it. That doesn't mean that the young man would get the same kind of a deal that a professional will get, but he'll get a piece of the action. Obviously, not everyone who walks in is going to have his idea read. Today, everybody and his brother is a television producer and they all have a package. There isn't anybody in the business who doesn't have a great idea for doing "Abner and Lum," which is a takeoff on "Lum and Abner." There isn't a person around who isn't a producer, or who isn't a creator, or who doesn't have an idea based on something that happened to their grandmother or their Aunt Tillie.

Along about the time we were developing "Hillbillies" we got into our first movie production. My first movie was "Boys' Night Out," with James Garner, Kim Novak, and Tony Randall. Two writers had come to see me with a four-page story outline of the movie. I thought it had a lot of promise and paid them five thousand dollars. It was a funny idea. I took it to Joe Levine, who at that time was releasing movies like "Hercules" and "Son of Hercules." He wanted to get into U.S. production. He read the outline in about three minutes and said O.K. We made the picture for two million four hundred thousand dollars and it was a very nice slick picture. It will gross more than five million.

That was my first taste of the movie business and I liked it. I took to it. I'm making four more pictures in 1963. And we're developing three more pilots for television. Our movies are going to be good, I think. As for releases, "The Wheeler Dealers" first, then "The Americanization of Emily," then Eric Ambler's "Light of Day," and finally an original that I wrote, "The Sandpiper." Without getting into all the details, I think that is going to be a good, sensitive picture.

I want to stay exactly where I am—a free and independent motion picture and television producer. I'm not tied up and I'm not tied down. I want to be literally and truly independent. I get my kicks from the wheeling and dealing, as well as the creative work. Buying properties, dealings with agents, negotiations with the distributors, all of it is fun. You have to know when to close a movie deal most of all. Timing is very critical in all areas, whether it be talent, subject matter, or releasing date for a picture.

I now travel more than I ever have, because movies are made all over the world. Last month I spent a couple of days in France, then London to set the Elizabeth Taylor deal for "Sandpiper" and back to Hollywood via New York, where we signed a three-picture deal with Carroll Baker. But no matter what they tell you, it's not the airplane or the electric light that man owes so much to, it's the telephone. At least to me. Ask anyone who knows me. Sometimes, they tell me, the phone looks like part of my hand. But it's important. In thirty seconds you can be anywhere in this country—a little longer, around the world. And a hell of a lot of our deals are done by phone.

Filmways can't grow into a studio because today studios are simply shops where independent producers work and make pictures to be released by the major companies. This is a city that has a lot of smog and a fairly nice climate, otherwise. It is inhabited by a lot of artists, producers, writers, and directors. Like any other business, some of these artists are good, some are bad, some are in the middle. There isn't any more Hollywood as Hollywood. The glitter, the glamour, everything that was necessary at one time—it just doesn't exist any more. This is good because serious picture-making is at a premium and the junk is at a minimum. It's bad because from an economic standpoint the thing that used to be a tremendous hook for people *was* the glitter and the glamour. And now it's largely a thing of the past.

In the old days the movie audiences could identify with these gods and goddesses. They used to be able to dream about this marvelous and glamorous life, but that was before the plane could get you there in four hours and the telephone could get you there for a dollar after nine o'clock at night and that was before big stars were dealing in collapsible corporations, and oil wells, and cattle ranches. It has been well publicized that movie stars today aren't movie stars—they're entrepreneurs. The stars are no longer love-gods and love-goddesses. They're businessmen worrying about capital gains and carry-backs and all the other tax jargon. The glitter that used to make movie-going an event is no longer. It used to be a side show, a circus. Not any more. It's the story that counts nowadays, not the glamour associated with the people.

But it still is a jungle, and for a young man to survive he's got to learn the rules of the jungle. He's got to understand that the odds on selling a finished pilot for a TV series is about one in fifteen. And pilots cost anywhere from a hundred thousand dollars on up to produce. And if you don't have network financing, forget it. The odds are around one in a hundred. The odds are higher in the movies.

First of all, you've got to have a property—an idea, a story, book rights, something tangible. This costs money unless you come up with the idea yourself. The movie rights on a best seller are incredibly expensive—no young man is going to have that kind of loot around. Then you have to have the confidence of management to turn over two or three million dollars to you. Then remember that the best properties on occasion have been ruined. And the men who run the studios, they're bright, very bright, but they've been burned before with great ideas which have turned out to be bombs.

So you have to have the idea and the confidence of management. One way to do it is to make the movie on a shoestring. A couple named Perry made "David and Lisa" on a shoestring. They formed a limited partnership and raised the dough dollar by dollar. They'll make a bundle out of their movie because it was good and intelligent and cheap. If a young guy is bright enough and he has a property he might go to Europe and find himself a co-production deal. But you need a bright agent or a sharp lawyer to pull off something like this.

Most of the young people in the movie industry today got their start as messenger boys, chorus boys, janitors, garbage men, anything in a studio. You've got to get in and be exposed to the business, to get the smell of the industry. There's no mystery to this business. The alert messenger boy or the bright studio runner is quick and learns a lot. He absorbs and gets the feel and instinct of the business. If he has some idea of the smell and feel of it and what makes it go then the next thing to do is to find an idea. Find a story and develop it to the point where it might only be ten or twelve pages. But if he's got it developed to the point that he can intrigue somebody with it, then he's moving. That's all.

It's a jungle, sure, but nobody's going to steal the idea. It doesn't happen. The kind of deal I would make with a beginner would be to make the picture and give the beginner a job as an associate producer at a weekly salary for the five months or so it takes to do the movie. And the kid would get a percentage of the profits.

I love the movie end of our company. The difference is that while I'm making the movies myself, I am not making the television shows. I'm involved in their creation and planning but in the movie end of the company I design, I create, I execute, and that's where the kicks are for me.

VII

Fred Hager is in one of today's most competitive businesses—the frozen-food plan. In a field in which numerous companies have suffered bankruptcies, Hager, Inc., has prospered to the point where Mr. Hager is, at thirty-six, a millionaire. He arrived in this country in 1951 with no money, a smattering of English, and the ability to work as a waiter.

FRED HAGER

I have certainly never regretted coming to America. I have a good business, I have a lovely family, and I have built a nice home in Westport, Connecticut. I was born in Switzerland thirty-six years ago, in a very small town about forty miles from Zürich. My parents had a little restaurant and a business. The business was actually a present to my father from one of my uncles. My father, however, was not a very good businessman. As a matter of fact, the business was losing money just about every year for more than twenty years, to a point where it eventually had to be sold at a price after which no money was left over.

I was only eighteen years old when my relatives had asked me to take over my father's business, because it was at that time at the verge of bankruptcy. My relatives had advanced my father quite a bit of money and it seemed that at this stage of the game they had lost all confidence and they implied that they would extend the credit somewhat if I took it over and if the business was completely under my own control. Although I was only eighteen, I had already some experience in the restaurant business. After all, I grew up in one and I had just finished serving a cook-apprenticeship. My father stepped in the background and I took the business over and it became quite successful. I initiated a few new ways of making money in the restaurant business in that town. One of them was that I started the first American Bar. I also started to advertise and induce husbands to take their wives out for dinner on Sundays, which created a little bit of an uproar in the beginning.

After a little more than a year of running this business and paying off some of the tremendous debt, we seemed to have trouble in the family because we did not all agree that the debts should be reduced. Some people thought that now there was a little money around, it should be spent, and since I did not agree with that thoroughly, I decided to strike out on my own and leave the business to my immediate family. This, in retrospect, proved to be the right thing for me and the way it worked out it also proved to be the end of my first job. When I left home I had about a thousand francs to my name and being an enterprising young man, I decided that there was quite a possibility that I could parlay that two hundred and fifty dollars in

American money into a fortune if I were a little lucky. I went to the nearest gambling casino in Italy—no gambling casinos are permitted in Switzerland. This casino was in Campioni. I had a lot to gain and a little to lose, so I lost a little, which made me quite broke.

I had saved just enough money to find my next job, where I worked as a waiter. The reason why I decided to work as a waiter rather than as a cook, which was my profession, was that I had felt that as a cook, even if I became a good cook, I could possibly be a chef, but I would never meet the right kind of people, whereas as a waiter, I had a good opportunity to meet all kinds of people and see a lot more about life in general. My first job as a waiter was actually in Geneva, Switzerland, in one of the first-class hotels there.

I then went to Lausanne, where I worked at the Palace Hotel, which just had been purchased by the Aga Khan. I had by now pretty much covered Switzerland, in my opinion, and I was anxiously looking across the border and wondered where I should go first. Fortunately the war was over and emigration visas were now available and I immediately took off for the Jersey General Islands, where I had secured a job by mail as a waiter. Travel facilities were not exactly ideal in 1945 in France and so it happened that when I arrived with great delay in Paris after taking many detours around bombed-out railroad bridges, I found that the boat that went from Samilow to the Jersey General Islands was only leaving every four weeks and it just had left. I decided it would be more interesting to wait in Paris the three weeks than at the small French town and quickly found that my money ran out completely. I found a job as a waiter in Paris in the very lively section of Place Pigalle. When I arrived in Jersey, I was amazed at the relatively poor conception that these Britishers had about food and good service. Of course, it was in 1945, and England has possibly never been known as a gourmet's paradise, but in 1945 it could be said that it was a gourmet's Inferno. Food was actually plentiful, but it was poorly prepared, especially in my opinion, since I had just left the employ of some of the world's finest hostelries.

There were several more Swiss in Jersey, actually, and we had quite a ball because of this easygoing life and the lack of demand of good service in these hotels. People were actually happy just as long as they got to eat on time and enough of it. They didn't even expect service, and they tipped very well. It was quite a happy crowd of people and they probably enjoyed their first vacation out of the British Islands after a long war and they took their happiness out on the waiters. For this reason I earned quite a bit of money during that time, which I saved. Right after the season I went into a program of getting myself a better education in a college in London. This was actually a Swiss mercantile college, supported partially by the Swiss Mercantile Society. I think that whatever I learned there helped me a great deal. I got familiar with a lot of financial terms, contracts, currencies, investments, et cetera.

After I left this school, I was looking for a job that would give me an opportunity to use my newly acquired skills, such as taking shorthand in French, English, and German. I was thinking of a job with the United Nations or possibly some international firm. After looking into several situations, I came to the conclusion that the salary that was available to me was not quite in line with the kind of income I was already used to as a waiter, and the idea of sitting behind a desk was a thought that I did not necessarily cherish at that stage of my career. So I gave up the whole idea and went to Holland to see if I could get a job on a boat so that I would have the opportunity to see the world a little bit.

It was not too easy to get a job in 1947 on a Dutch boat if you were Swiss. There were a great many people, especially the Dutch themselves, who would have gone to work on a boat like the *Nieuw Amsterdam* for a trip to New York, almost without compensation. The intangible fringe benefits in connection with cigarettes and nylon stockings were far outweighing the advantages of the weekly paycheck. I was actually spending a couple of weeks in Rotterdam trying to get a job at the *Nieuw Amsterdam*, seeing the hiring officer daily, and wearing him down with my persistence, and while I was sitting around in the office passing the time, I was studying Dutch very intensely. I think the fact that it took me only two weeks to learn Dutch reasonably well must have impressed him, for against all odds I finally did get the job.

I was extremely excited to see New York the first time. I had read so much about the life in New York with opportunities in America in general and from an untold number of pictures which I had seen, I could just picture the New York skyline before we even saw it. The hustle and bustle in New York really fascinated me, although I had but a few hours' leave, and somehow I was thinking if I only could get the visa to stay in the United States on a permanent basis. A few trips later I met a very friendly psychiatrist from Philadelphia. He was a delegate to some kind of an international psychiatrist convention in London, and after serving him and his party of six for the full extent of the trip from New York to Southampton, he asked me if I would like to go to the United States. He followed right up with saying that if I did, he knew that I would be very successful there.

I told him that it wasn't as easy as he thought because I needed a sponsor according to the American immigration laws who would guarantee that I would not become a financial burden to the public. This means that if I would run out of funds that person would have to support me, to which the doctor replied, "If that's all you're concerned about, consider yourself going to America." I didn't hear anything from the doctor until several weeks later I received a letter from him and several enclosures of legal papers applying for a visa and an affidavit of support by the doctor. I was very happy about this and made arrangements to emigrate to the United States as soon as my quota came up.

I actually had little money at that time and for economic reasons I took a freighter to Boston. From there I went by Greyhound to New York. I found it very, very cold. It was just about two days after Christmas. I made a careful analysis of my assets, which amounted to one hundred eighty dollars, of which I invested thirty-five in a Greyhound ticket to Miami. I thought that if things were rough, the balance of the money would last a lot longer in a warm climate than in a cold one—in an emergency one could, after all, sleep outside and hotels were one thing I didn't have money for.

In Miami I was able to get sleeping accommodations (if you could call it that) for five dollars a week right in a beach-front hotel. If I remember correctly, it was around Eighth Street and it was the Edgewater Beach. My quarters were downstairs next to the boiler room. There were several other cots there, but I didn't mind that very much. After all, it was the first time that I had such lovely weather at a time when it was usually freezing everywhere else.

I soon found myself a job as a waiter in a steak house, which started at four in the afternoon, and I had practically every day up to three to myself on the beach. My overhead was extremely low. My breakfast consisted always of a pound of bananas, about seven cents, about five oranges, which were less than a quarter, and I took that back to the beach and then wouldn't eat anything else until I was starting to work in the steak house. So my total living expenses were about seven dollars a week. I saved almost all of the difference between what I was making and what my living expenses were and after the season, I went to New York.

I wanted to go to work as a waiter, but I could not get the required certificate of health in New York to take a job as a waiter because I had a cancerous-type wound on my left forearm, which at that time they thought it may be cancer and sent me to the cancer clinic. Actually it was a sore that was created by my watch which I never removed when swimming in the salt water for several hours in the morning, and once it was open it just would not heal. It healed up soon, though, and I took a job in Larchmont in Westchester County where, for some reason, nobody asked me about a certificate of health. Actually the job I had taken in Larchmont was that of a dishwasher first, simply because there was nothing else open. I was promoted, however, within days, to busboy, and even at that, they thought I had more potential and a few days later I became a waiter. At that time, however, my wound was completely healed and I got myself a job at the Waldorf Astoria as a waiter. Actually it wasn't as easy as that to get a job at the Waldorf for me because I did not belong to the union and the Waldorf was a closed shop. I had to do an awful lot of talking and pull a few tricks, but eventually I was in there anyway.

The Waldorf Astoria was the place of my longest job. I worked at the Waldorf for a full eight months. I probably wouldn't have worked there that long if it didn't have too many restaurants. I worked at the Sert Room, the Empire Room, Peacock Alley, the Palm Bar, the Starlight Roof, the third-floor banquet department, and on the fourth-floor rooms. It was at that time that I had actually decided to make a career in the restaurant business and in order to do that I embarked on a plan to work in as many restaurants as possible in the shortest possible time. This took me from New York to Atlantic City to Spring Lake to White Sulphur Springs, back to Miami, to Houston, Texas, to Chicago, where I worked in at least twenty different places. Usually, when I knew where all the silverware was, I felt it was time to leave.

I struck out on my own in Miami and opened a restaurant called "Freddie's." It was a small restaurant in downtown Miami, where, according to the very smooth real estate operator who sold me the deal, business was going wild all year round. I actually took this restaurant right at the end of the season of Miami Beach and downtown, according to the rosy predictions of this salesman, business was actually bigger in the summer than in the winter. Up to this time in my life I had not been exposed very much to glib salesmanship, and I was taken for a ride. Looking back to this venture which cost me a few thousand dollars, I think it was one of the best things that could have happened to me, because it happened when I was very young, about twenty-six years old, and I could start over again and learn by the mistake.

When I sold the restaurant, I sold it to a jeweler next door for fifty dollars, and I took all the groceries, such as potatoes, spaghetti, tomatoes, purées, and things like that, and peddled them off at some restaurants at half price. After making two or three stops, someone must have called the police, because I was picked up, taken downtown and made to explain where I got all those groceries which I was selling so cheaply. After identifying myself and taking them down to my place, we all had a good laugh and the police left me alone so that I could peddle off the rest of my groceries.

At this time I had actually changed some of my views about the restaurant business. I knew I could make good money working as a waiter, but to own a restaurant had lost an awful lot of its glamour for me. I considered it pretty much of a peanut business, especially considering the type of restaurants that I could have managed to own at that time with my limited funds. Actually, knowing about the restaurant business what I know today, it is not surprising to me that the majority of the small restaurants have difficulties in showing a profit and also have difficulties in obtaining credit. Considering this, I started to try jobs connected with selling as a sideline.

It would take me too long to list all the different jobs that I had held at that time as a part-time salesman, sometimes, and sometimes as a full-time salesman. Not knowing anything about selling at the time, the time invested in selling on a strictly commission basis was usually depleting my financial resources, and when I had a full-time job for a while, I usually had to go back as a waiter where at least I always had a definite income. I tried to read every book that I could get hold of on salesmanship. This no doubt helped me a great deal. Actually Frank Bettger's book, *How I Raised Myself from Failure to Success in Selling*, became my Bible.

I had some other handicaps at the time. One of the more important ones being a severe accent in my speech. This wasn't really a handicap except in my mind, but I always felt ill at ease when I was trying to make a sales presentation. It was at this time that I enrolled in a Dale Carnegie course for public speaking and I do believe that the training and more so, possibly, the psychological impact of getting over the fear of speaking in public, completely eliminated my complex about my accent. If anything, I learned to use it to my advantage. I was now a pretty fair salesman and actually was making a living selling on a strictly commission basis. What I really needed was something to burn my bridges behind me and tear myself away from the restaurant business.

I did something like that when I worked at the West-chester Country Club in Rye, where I worked as a waiter. I got into a disagreement with the shop steward about the breaks I was getting as far as rotating the more profit-able tables with other waiters. This fellow thought that for a kid of my age I was pretty fresh, especially when this job was supposed to be one of the best jobs in West-chester County. I said that I needed him less than I needed a hole in the head and he said, "If you walk off this job now during the season, you will not get any more jobs through this local." I don't know the number now of this local—it was a restaurant union local in Mount Vernon. But I did walk off the job. This finished me as a member in good standing with the union in Westchester County. Of course, I couldn't have cared less, but still I tried to secure myself a job over the weekends where I thought I could pick up maybe fifty or sixty dollars in a restaurant to complement my income from selling, which I did now during the day on a commission basis.

At that time there was a restaurant in Mount Vernon called the Studio Club. It was a well-known, expensive restaurant. I believe it is out of business now. The head-waiter there was known to be some kind of a nut, and few union waiters would have stood for the kind of treat-ment he was dishing out. He was one of these old-time bosses—his word was the law and there was no room for argument. He was always right and the waiter was always wrong. Before I got a job there I had an interview with the headwaiter, who was a Frenchman, and I talked to him in French and I was hired.

I did get a big group of tables to serve which I felt

was just a few tables too many. I told the headwaiter that
if these tables were occupied, I could never take care of
them properly, especially with the intricate menu they
had, and he said to me, "Don't worry about it. The place
won't fill up, and I gave you some tables that are usually
not taken anyway." It didn't work out that way, though,
and the tables filled up. I got a party of eight in addition
to three parties I was already serving, and the man who
was apparently footing the bill approached me with a
ten-dollar bill and said, "Here, you can have half of this.
Take care of us and I will give you the other half later."
First of all I resented this approach, which I considered
humiliating, and secondly, I knew he wouldn't get any
good service simply because of the number of people that
I had to take care of. I gave him this half bill back and
said, "Why don't you give me your tip when you leave
because then you'll know how much you should give me
and I can assure you right now that service today is not
going to be too good; there are too many people and I
can only take one party after another in the succession
they came in."

The man was quite upset by what he called my "arro-
gance," called the headwaiter over, told him what I told
him, after which the headwaiter asked me to apologize
and called me all kinds of names in French. I said to myself, "Well, this is a good time to burn my bridges." I
took off my long apron—we were wearing these French
aprons going all the way to the floor in connection with a
dinner jacket and I offered the apron to the headwaiter,
saying, "Here is my apron. You can have it. I'm finished."
I took off my badge and gave it to the gentleman who had

caused all this trouble and said, "Why don't you help the headwaiter serving this party," after which I briskly walked out of the restaurant, not taking any pay. I am sure I was now on the blacklist because I couldn't even get a non-union job. But this is really what I wanted. I didn't want to get back in the restaurant business. I don't think I'm cut out to be a waiter.

Fortunately it was at this time that I started to meet with some moderate success in selling. The job I held was that of an independent dealer with Century Metalcraft in Mount Vernon, selling cooking equipment, pots, and pans. I was very happy when I actually was able to make a good week's pay as a salesman, especially because only a couple of months ago I had been interviewed at the Statler Hotel in New York by some representatives of the *Encyclopædia Britannica* where I was told that I couldn't get a job, even on a commission basis, since I didn't have the educational background to make a salesman who could sell encyclopedias.

One day, giving a party demonstration in waterless cooking, I found I had some competition. The lady who was giving the party had invited another salesman who was giving a presentation of his food-freezer plan to the whole group while I was washing up the dishes. Much to my chagrin he had taken down payments from everybody and when I was going to see these people in connection with a sale, they had no money left for down payments for me. I thought that maybe I was in the wrong business and immediately got myself a job with that food plan. The idea of selling a freezer with food appealed to me greatly, but at the time I found out soon that there were few companies that were actually trying to sell an honest program with good food. Most of them were interested mostly in the sale of a freezer. They were actually not even in the food business.

I therefore conceived the idea of trying to talk a bank into lending me a little bit of money to start a business of my own. The credit that I got was so limited that I could only sell myself, because if I had hired any people, I would have been under-capitalized. I was making quick progress, though, and it didn't take me long to have my credit line increased, which enabled me to hire some salesmen, after which progress was made quite fast. I actually had the bank discount the freezer installment notes from me and the food notes and they did take quite a heavy reserve against this contingent liability so that I had just about enough money from the proceeds to pay the commission of the salesmen.

This forced me to keep my overhead so low that I had built very good equities in my reserves. The food I had contracted for with a reliable food supplier, and because I paid him cash and I endorsed installment notes, I had good control over the quality. It did not take me long, however, to realize that even this kind of control was not adequate and I started to build a little place where I could process foods and freeze them so I could be in the food business myself. In order to do that I purchased a piece of property in Fairfield, Connecticut, which was actually formerly used as a dump by McKesson and Robbins. I purchased it for five thousand dollars, with one thousand down. On that site I put a trailer where I took up living quarters and I also used it as an office. Now I negotiated for someone to put up a small building and because I didn't have much cash I had to arrange to borrow all the money. The builder asked me for at least a five-thousand-dollar down payment for a building which was going to cost twenty-five thousand, or else to have clear title to the land on which I still owed now four thousand dollars.

Well, I could not give him the money for the down payment, so I managed to borrow the four thousand dollars from some party in New York at a fantastic amount of interest. As a matter of fact, I signed a five-thousand-dollar note to get four thousand cash and paid six per cent interest on five thousand, for twelve months, which figured out to an interest rate of thirty-two per cent. This is how some people get around lending you money at exorbitant rates by giving you less than the face of the note and charging you a small interest. Anyway, I was glad I got the money, even at thirty-two per cent, and fortunately I managed to pay off that note at the end of the year. From there on, things went quite rapid.

Sales in the first year were around three hundred thousand dollars, some five hundred thousand dollars in the second year, close to a million dollars in the third, a million and a half the fourth year, to in excess of three million dollars in 1963. We are now quite solidly established in the frozen food business and our next phase of business is going to be one of diversification. To achieve that goal we have already now completed research and development for a new merchandising program which will feature a revolutionary method for heating prepared gourmet dishes in a matter of one or two minutes.

My experience as a chef has been helpful in the supervision of creating a full line of gourmet dishes which are prepared at a new commissary recently built by us and are then distributed in a frozen state. I do believe that the trend in this country is toward more convenience and, therefore, these dishes which require only to be put in an electronic oven, I believe, will eventually meet great consumer acceptance. Of course, these dinners that we are putting out cannot in any way be compared to TV dinners. They are quality dishes which can be served at fine restaurants.

Actually, the way I envision the future of this concept, I can see restaurants selling exclusively a wide variety, maybe as many as forty different dishes, of recipes from every corner of the world. The inherent savings in operation costs related to labor, profit control, and lack of waste are so obvious that a great many authorities in the food service field today are convinced that a few years from now more than fifty per cent of all meals consumed in public eating places will be prepared by central commissary-type food manufacturing organizations, rather than individual small kitchens.

When I am asked why I have succeeded where others have failed in our field, it is always difficult for me to give a good answer and usually I shrug it off, "with luck." However, I do believe that hard work, persistence, general enthusiasm, self-assurance, salesmanship, and a fair judgment are some of the qualities that are necessary to accomplish more than the average. Maybe the most important single character trait in my opinion is the ability to save money even though you have little to spend. For a great many years I had always made it my business to put a small portion of my income away and many times when I needed money in the worst way I always had some place from which I could draw a little bit more.

I also believe that it is impossible always to succeed with any project that one starts. Success, in addition to all those factors mentioned, has to be combined with a program that makes business sense, and while one has many times an idea about a way of making a lot of money, one has to keep trying because one has to try usually several times to come up with something that pays off. I think that if we were now not engaged in several other projects, we would not be able to go ahead simply because in business standing still is going backwards and because people change, products change, and the wants of people change.

One does not have to succeed with everything one tries in order to become successful, but one has to have the stomach to fail and try again and fail and try again, because by the mere law of averages, the one who tries the most is likely to hit sooner or later. When you ask me for advice on what I would do if I had to start from scratch again, I would say, become a good salesman first, because there isn't any phase in business that is not in some way connected with selling, be it the selling of some investor or some banks on lending you money, or selling some supplier in giving you credit, or selling some people on working for you, or selling the product itself, or be able to guide the people who are in charge of selling, which is the most important phase of a business such as ours. Of course, I am speaking about a commercial business such as ours, but if you are a professional inventor, you certainly, if you're lucky, will make money without having any other qualities, but today there are few people actually making money on inventions alone. You also have to sell the invention.

My last piece of advice would be: after you have mastered salesmanship, get into a field of endeavor that you really love, not just like, so that you can get excited about it, because if you are excited about it, hard work does not bother you, you don't even feel it. Your business becomes a hobby, which truly it should be. In this spirit you will be able to overcome a lot of things that if you are just an employee you could not muster the energy to overcome, and I think that I am not exaggerating when I say that most really successful organizations that have been built with moderate means have attained their success because of the genuine enthusiasm with which their management has gone about to build the organization. And one last piece of advice is: a lot of well-made plans of mice and men can fail, and therefore, you should not commit everything you have to one thing, even though it may look tremendous. I think that one should always hedge a bet.

In summarizing, I am certainly convinced that the opportunities in this country are still there for everyone who can see them, but I do think there are less people today who can see them because maybe today we are a little bit less rugged individuals than the Americans were who have actually built this continent and too many of us believe the cliché that "there are no more opportunities."

VIII

William A. Romain is another business executive who struggled through the Depression. He was raised in Detroit and eventually reached a pinnacle for many Detroit youths—the Ford Motor Company. He now is president of the Novo Corporation.

WILLIAM A. ROMAIN

My father was a young European immigrant who came to Pennsylvania and worked in the coal mines at the turn of the century. My mother's father also was a coal miner. My parents got married in 1910 and in 1919, two weeks after I was born, they moved to a small town in Illinois called Carlinville. My father did fairly well at his work. He operated what was then a rather glamorous piece of equipment, a diamond drill. I remember we were relatively wealthy because in 1923 my father bought a Dodge for one thousand seven hundred dollars. It was one of the first sedans in town. My father earned something like one hundred fifty dollars a week, which were good wages in that particular field.

When I was about four years old, the mine closed down. The family moved to Detroit where my father went to work as an auto worker for Ford. He worked at different jobs for Ford and in his spare time he tried to cash in on the land boom. He lost his shirt at that, and then the Depression came. There were no jobs, and I guess that my father worked six months out of the year. Things were very difficult with the mortgage hanging over the family. I remember my father walking for miles to save a few cents by buying wholesale meat for the family. We were never hungry. I can't plead that kind of poverty at home, but we always were fearing the threat of tomorrow's uncertainty. One Christmas I wrote a letter to Santa Claus because it looked like I wasn't going to get any presents. I got presents that year, through the courtesy of the Good Fellows of Detroit.

I was the only child in the family up until 1931. Then, rather late in life, my mother had a daughter that year and another daughter in 1933. So there were three children in the family.

My family thought I should get a good Catholic education, so I was sent to school at Saint Theresa's, which is a Catholic parochial school in Detroit. The school was in the upper middle-class strata, and some of the kids were quite wealthy. I couldn't seem to understand why my family had to live on a day-to-day basis while other children seemed to have whatever they wanted—toys and plenty of clothes. These children obviously reflected their parents' financial status, and I couldn't quite understand why some kinds were "haves," and others, like myself, were "have nots." I was determined that my children would lead lives like these youngsters and that I wouldn't have my family go through depression periods as I did. There must have been a reason why that difference existed, and I was determined to spend my life in the "have" group.

I resented being classified as poor because my family never said we were poor, or destitute. They said you couldn't have this or you couldn't have that because of economic conditions, but it was always a fight internally to better themselves. It wasn't resentment at all. In fact, I resented more some of my classmates who would always say they were poor and using this as an excuse that they couldn't do this or that because of their poorness. They used their poverty as a defense.

All this time, I had been formulating a plan for my future education. I wanted to learn shorthand and typing but the principal ridiculed the idea. She said these subjects were only for girls. But I thought that these skills might be a shortcut to the executive office I had in mind so I transferred to a public school. Most ambitious young men in those days went to work behind a machine at Ford, fully intending to work their way up. But within a year these ambitious young men usually turned into robots— through a sort of mechanical brainwash. I saw this happen to many friends and relatives. And I didn't want this to happen to me. This becoming a robot seemed to be a general pattern. Working your way up from the bottom didn't seem to be the answer except to a very few, and then by chance.

Everyone dreams of success, but merely wishing for his ship to come in seldom works out except in Horatio Alger stories. The way to do it is to spell out a definite plan which both the conscious and the subconscious minds can go to work on and realize. I was then developing a twenty-five year blueprint plan for my life in business. The blueprint was a single page and it looked like the so-called organizational chart. The steps in the blueprint started with my getting a job as a clerk, then a secretary, then a junior executive, and finally the presidency and chairmanship of a corporation. I then had in mind an automotive firm because of my Detroit background.

I graduated from Tappan, the junior high school I had been attending, and went to the Detroit High School of Commerce, which had the cream of the crop of teachers and was worth the forty-five minute bus ride I had to take to get to school. I had taken typing at Tappan, and at Commerce I took shorthand. I was the only boy in the shorthand class out of forty girls. I was a class officer in high school and editor of the school newspaper. I finished high school in July of 1937, and had intended to go to Wayne State University in Detroit on a scholarship. I went out looking for work to earn income enough to pay for a year of college. But those plans were changed when my father was killed by a hit-and-run driver in January of 1938.

I had had one job at U.S. Rubber as a shipping clerk on the midnight shift at forty-five cents an hour, six days a week. My classification called for a higher rate, so I asked for a raise. My supervisor said, "If you get me a raise, I'll get you one." I took him seriously and went to the executive offices and tried to get the raise for him. I didn't realize he had been joking. The people in the executive offices took it as a joke, too. But my supervisor didn't think it was funny. He fired me. That was the first and last time I've ever asked for a raise. Those were still recession days, and I was out of work from November of 1937 through April of 1938. In between, my father had died. There was a little insurance which covered the burial but then with the mortgage on the house and two young sisters it became a desperate necessity for me to find employment to earn decent money as the head of the family.

I had been trying for some time to get a job at Ford, but it was very difficult to get in there even to fill out an application. One way you could be interviewed was to buy a new Ford car. The dealer would then give you an introduction to obtain employment. The only thing was when your payments were through so was your job, and of course I didn't have enough money even to make a down payment on a car. What I finally did was have a friend of mine who worked at Ford get me some official, engraved Ford stationery. I filled out a letter of introduction and scribbled an illegible name at the bottom. It got me in the door. I was a little nervous at doing something like that. I suppose it was a gamble, but what could I lose? The worst thing that could happen is that they would send me home. Once I was in I filled out an application blank and was sent to Camp Legion, the idea for which had occurred to Henry Ford only a week earlier.

Camp Legion was one of Ford's brainchilds. He didn't think that the farmers needed Federal assistance. He thought it would spoil them. Ford had talked to F.D.R. and said that the American farmer was an individualist and was able to work out his own problems. F.D.R. laughed at this and said, "Why don't you go ahead and do that to your workers?" Ford said, "I'll get a bunch of boys and put them on my land, give them seed and tools, and they'll make money and still have some left over." And before the week was out he had sixty-five boys together who were going to work at his farm at two dollars a day with room and board plus a bonus if the camp showed a profit. I'd say only a few of us were underprivileged. The balance of the boys were well-to-do and were just in it for the summer vacation.

The camp was built and run on a semi-military basis, much like the C.C.C. Instead of a bugle, we had a Ford V-8 horn. The food was excellent. In the morning we would line up for inspection. Looking back on it, it was almost one big picnic. Ford used to come out and have breakfast with us once a week. Generally speaking, he was somewhat aloof. Now and then he would take a specific interest in some youngster but most of the time he stayed away from us.

I was assigned to the farm group and we did various farming, one of which was cultivating corn. It was a rather senseless move, because actually you could take a tractor and a cultivator and do the thing in an afternoon. Actually, there wasn't enough work for so many boys. There must have been thirty of us to a row.

When you're put in a group like that, you have to make an effort to stand out, to do just a little better than the next fellow to get the recognition if you want to move ahead of the rest. So I just decided to hoe faster and get in front of the group. At the other end of the field was Verl Brown, the assistant employment manager of Ford, who was assigned as camp director. Brown would visit the camp daily and on this one occasion he happened to see me hoeing with no one else in sight. He asked me what I was doing there and I explained that the others just couldn't keep up. He said I should get back with the group so I started hoeing another row back. The next day I was promoted to the camp powerhouse in charge of maintenance. At the end of six months we each received a bonus of one hundred sixty dollars. My hard work seemed to pay off. During my stay at Camp Legion I edited the camp paper and later became assistant manager of the produce market.

The idea was that at the finish of camp we would be given any job in the company for which we qualified. When it came time for this, I realized that I didn't even have the experience to work on the assembly line. And clerical positions at Ford were few and far between. I did want a job as a private secretary to one of the executives, but I didn't think that was an end in itself. The end goal that I had with my twenty-five year plan was to head up an industrial complex. I figured that even if I was qualified for the assembly line, I'd be getting into the same thing I was trying to avoid earlier in life, that is, being stuck behind some complex machine as a specialist. But it turned out that Ford had a training school, which paid four-forty per day for eight hours of work and then you were sent to the Ford apprentice school for a couple of hours after work to study blueprint reading, mathematics, and so forth. That sounded pretty good so I took it. Some of the boys ended up as test-track drivers, and others ended up as tool makers or die makers.

Meanwhile my family was getting by. While at Camp

Legion I had been making twelve dollars a week. I gave my mother ten of that, which was enough to keep the family from going hungry for those six months. My mother picked up part-time work as a domestic worker, but that was quite infrequent. I wouldn't say it was a real struggle, but then again, it wasn't the most comfortable way to live. We made payments on the mortgage. In fact, when I got the bonus at the end of camp we caught up with all the back mortgage payments and that was where the bulk of the one hundred sixty dollars went. So when the offer of the Ford training school at four-forty a day came along, it looked fairly good for the very tight budget we were on at the time.

The formal training school consisted of a four-month term during which high-school graduates were assigned to various departments such as machining, electrical, metallurgy, et cetera. I was assigned as a follow-up man in Ford's Department N–640, which was the place where the oddball things had to be done. It was the kind of place where I spent half my time chasing down small quantities of copper tubing, plastics, and various metals which were needed in various sections of the factory. Then, one day I was sent over to the executive offices where I took a dictation test from one of the officials. A gentleman came in and introduced himself as George Sherman and said Ford had some ideas cooking in the tractor field and that I would hear further from him.

I was sent back to training school and after hearing nothing further for several weeks, I got restless and requested a transfer. I found myself transferred to "Michigan Dealers"—a department where all of the small parts

were sent to Ford dealers in Michigan. "Michigan Dealers" was a catch-all for misfits from the Service Department. It was a haven for punch-drunk fighters, ex-fugi-
tives, parolees, retired or fired policemen—the people who
couldn't do a normal day's work but for whom the Ford
Service Department felt obligated to pay six dollars a day
in 1939.

My assignment was to type labels for the packages
going out and I wasn't too welcome in the department in-
asmuch as I was replacing an old fellow who had broken
his hand and had used the hunt-and-peck system in
typing.

I had been a runner-up in the 1937 Detroit typewriting
contest, and could type seventy-six words per minute. It
soon became apparent that I could typewrite in an hour
or two what the other gent took eight hours to do on the
hunt-and-peck method. This didn't make me too popular
in the department; I typed like the devil anyway. Not to
take over my predecessor's job, but because I knew I was
not going to remain there very long. I finished my first
day's work in about an hour and then confounded the
department supervisor by asking for something to do.

He said that once or twice a month a general mailing
was made to all Michigan dealers and that I could prepare
a few sets of labels in advance. After a few weeks, however, and a couple of hundred sets of labels, I began to
run out of storage space. I presented the problem to the
department supervisor, who came up with a solution. He
told me to destroy the labels and start all over. I did this,
but then tried to type twice as fast.

I was nineteen years old at the time and I suppose I

thought that if I made enough of a splash in that department, they'd be forced to get rid of me and put me in some other position. Finally, on May 1, 1939, George Sherman called for me and that was the last I saw of the Michigan Dealers department.

Sherman explained that Harry Ferguson, an inventor from Belfast, Ireland, had come to this country and had been introduced to Henry Ford by Sherman's brother. Ferguson sold Ford on an idea for a new type of Ford tractor. Ferguson would handle the distribution of the tractor.

Now, Ford had been in the tractor business in the early twenties but he dropped out because the tractor had the quirk of turning over and generally killing the operator. It was not too popular.

Sherman had a small plant in Evansville, Indiana, making a wheelless plow and then Ferguson came along with a hydraulic means of lifting the implements. Up until then, the conventional way of plowing was to pull the plow. However, this tractor was the first wheelless type that theoretically had automatic depth control by hydraulic pressure. It was a breakthrough in agriculture and the Ferguson-Sherman Manufacturing Company was formed to market the Ford tractor. I joined the organization as a private secretary to George Sherman. He couldn't hire any girls or women because of the Ford policy of prohibiting females in the Rouge plant.

When I was with Sherman it became obvious that I could not just drop my job and go to college to get a college education so I tried to get the equivalent of it by a three-year correspondence course in accounting. After two years in the course I requested a transfer to the accounting department because Mr. Sherman left the company and I was afraid of being frozen in the secretarial category. It's a rather awkward position. If a man is good at it, he'll probably be kept at it. And if he's too good, of course, he's not happy. I worked with the accounting department and had a few small promotions.

In the meantime World War Two broke out and, while farm tractors were vital to some degree, it seemed either mark time for the duration or wait for Uncle Sam to call you into service. At the outset, I was classified 3–A, head of a household. I was approached by one of the manufacturing executives at Ford who offered me a supervisory position in the salvage department. This entailed the actual accounting of the ordnance projects such as the Ford M4 tanks, armored cars, and the Sperry bombsights.

My job consisted of keeping tabs on all the scrap material which did not go into the finished product. Every ounce of unused material had to be accounted for because it was Government property with the usual seven-copy method of bureaucratic record-keeping. I probably had thirty people under me at the time, most of whom were inexperienced young women. After the war really got serious, I wanted to get into the service rather than just maintain a war job, and since my mother had secured a job working for Ford as an assembly worker the family fortunes were in fairly good shape. Her work was very light; they even had grandmothers working, and with overtime she was living quite well. Today she is enjoying the California sunshine.

What I wanted to do was get into the V–12 program or

something similar to it. There I could get additional education. I was not accepted, however, because of my vision, and within ten days of the turndown I received my greetings from Uncle Sam. I happened to remark to the examining psychiatrist at the induction center that war was a "hell of a way" for civilized people to settle their international differences. It seemed to me that this should be done over bargaining tables rather than people butchering each other. The psychiatrist accused me of being a conscientious objector. But when I told him I preferred doing something constructive rather than destructive, he said, "I've got just the thing for you, the Navy's Seabees."

I spent twenty-eight months in the service, building bridges, airfields, et cetera, from October, 1943, to February, 1946, in the Pacific Theater, and almost lost my life in the Philippines—but not in action. A giant centipede bit me and the poison had no known antidote. The doctor said that nothing could be done about it, you simply had to lie down for four hours and you either pulled through or you didn't. In about four hours the excruciating pain went away and I was still alive. I couldn't get up for two days, but everyone said I was a lucky guy; even natives had died from centipede bites.

I guess we were all dreamers about what we wanted to do when the war was over. It's hard to put into words because wartime is an artificial situation, and it's difficult to really plan rationally because war is abnormal. I guess everyone deep in his mind knew that the war would end and we would be the victors and that the new postwar world would be just as good as the one we left. But those are assumptions and it was difficult to nail things down on a concrete basis until the latter part of the war when I seriously began to think again about where I was going and what I was going to do. But I continued my studies during the war, reading anything I could get my hands on and taking courses through the Armed Forces Institute. I didn't lose any of my zest during the war. My plan was postponed a bit, but that's all. I was discharged from the service in February, 1946, at Great Lakes.

Before I got out, I got a note from the former treasurer of Ferguson, Tom Murphy, who said that George Sherman was working on a project that he thought I might find interesting, so while I was waiting to be discharged I contacted Sherman. He had been working on the design and development of a tractor after he left Ferguson, and felt that the vast plants of the war effort would be idle after the war and that the automakers would have to diversify in order to utilize their investment.

I gave Sherman a call. He came out to the house and told me what he had planned. He had taken his tractor overdrive transmission and redesigned it to fit into the Ford transmission housing, which doubled the gear speed and became a very much needed accessory. His idea was to go into the production and sale of this transmission. I was offered a job as corporate secretary and a directorship in the firm. Sherman thought highly of me and was a man who always believed in giving a youth—I was twenty-seven years old—a break. He was childless and looked upon me as sort of a business son, and there weren't too many people willing to start from scratch or on a shoe-string. We raised fifty-five thousand dollars to capitalize the company. I invested one thousand dollars of my savings, which was practically all the money I had, and George Sherman put in twenty thousand dollars—every cent he had. About thirty other people invested amounts varying from five hundred to five thousand dollars each.

The company did very well. It couldn't help but be a success, because there was a tremendous pent-up demand for farm equipment and the transmission made the tractor more versatile. In fact, they are still being used by tractors today in some models. All we did was farm out the machining, assemble the units, and ship them out on a mail-order basis. A year and a half later the pipelines were filled and we had to develop new products.

At first we rented a small vacant store, where we had about ten engineers and draftsmen perfecting the details of the transmission. I wore many hats: receptionist, purchasing agent, assistant to the president. I also was the man who talked to Dun and Bradstreet on credit ratings, and set up the company's accounting system. In 1948, we recapitalized and went on an over-the-counter basis. There were about six hundred shareowners, and we raised two hundred seventy thousand dollars in order to acquire new plant facilities and also to provide for the work on new products—which flopped.

I think we were a little spoiled by our initial success and didn't plan carefully enough. We developed what we called the "Farmcrafter," a combination drill press and grinding wheel in an attachment which would fit on tractors. Theoretically, we thought it might be a natural because the farmer then could put one of these rigs on his equipment and be able to repair or sharpen his tools in the field—sort of a do-it-yourself thing. We overlooked completely the fact that the farmer was quite prosperous at the time and instead of taking the time to do this, either got a new tool or sent it to the blacksmith. I don't think we sold five hundred of the things.

Finally, we found a small company, Wain-Roy Corporation, which had developed a hydraulic power digger. Wain-Roy didn't have a sales organization, however, so we arranged a joint engineering-manufacturing arrangement, and marketed the products exclusively through the Sherman sales organization. This hydraulic digger replaced the old-fashioned pick and shovel operation in the excavation of basements, pipelines, septic tanks, et cetera. Today this is a fifty-million-dollar-a-year industry, with a number of companies engaged in manufacturing the equipment.

In 1954, George Sherman died of a heart attack without designating a successor and our board of directors was divided on the company's future operation. Some of the shareholders wanted to sell out to one of the farm equipment manufacturers, but I was convinced that we had the management depth to carry on, and Mrs. Sherman, with controlling interest, agreed to continue. A year later, however, she decided it would be safer to diversify her holdings and notified me that she planned to sell her stock in the company. Mrs. Sherman's attorney thought that since she had the controlling interest, she could sell her shares at a good price since the buyer then would have controlling interest.

When active negotiations opened, she was offered two hundred fifty thousand dollars, or three dollars per share, at a time when it was only selling at two twenty-five, and this looked very attractive to her since she was not very wealthy. She agreed, however, to give me time to try to match the offer when I told her I was sure that I could distribute the stock among four or five investors. I thought it would be simple to raise the money right in Detroit, but after approaching people with our balance sheets, operating statements, and projections, I discovered that I'd been sadly mistaken. Even those people which my bank suggested might be interested, turned me down.

I couldn't raise a dime locally and that hurt because I had spent so much time in community activities. I was a director and chairman of the United Foundation, and a member of the Chamber of Commerce, the Boy Scouts Executive Council, the Republican Party, Boys' Clubs, and was involved in many other such activities. I wouldn't characterize myself as a joiner, but I've always looked upon extracurricular activities as a good training ground for junior executives. Further, a businessman has a moral obligation to his community in lending the know-how of his leadership.

Despite my connections, I couldn't raise the two hundred fifty thousand dollars locally because the people still thought of us as a tool-and-die operation. We had a national reputation, though, and a national sales organization, so I started telephoning some shareholders and distributors who handled our products. I also called up an investment banker in New York and spelled out the whole situation; that's how I raised the money.

Sales were about three million dollars a year in 1954 when I became president, and in June of 1960 when Sherman Products was sold to Ford, annual sales were about seven million dollars.

We had, in effect, converted a farm tractor into an industrial machine, and Ford decided to get into that market themselves and began designing and making their own equipment. So, it seemed to be only a matter of time before we would merge with a larger, stronger company or else just dry up. We sold for about two and a half million dollars and, although the sale didn't make me a millionaire, I would say that it amounted to a good investment for myself and the other stockholders. Sherman was too small. We were not in a position to design and sell our own tractor.

In 1959, quite some time before we sold out to Ford, I met Walter Bronston, head of Industrial Enterprises, Inc., a company with a highly diversified line. This included heavy-duty overhead traveling cranes at Milwaukee Crane, bridge fabricating at Vincennes Steel, air cleaners at United Air Cleaner, rolled-form automotive parts at Mitchell Specialty, housewares at Pennant, hauling and drive-away automotive parts at Fleet Carrier Corporation, film storage at Bonded Services, plus a few research and development projects. The company had been losing money. Bronston sensed operational problems due to stiffening competition and felt the management structure needed strengthening.

Walter offered me the executive vice-presidency of Industrial Enterprises in October of 1959 and I was interested in the proposition because it sounded like a real challenge. After we sold Sherman, I spent two weeks with Walter visiting all of the divisions and getting the feel of the company. There was a great deal of work to be done, but basically there was something solid in the organization. I took the job with a promise of consideration of stock options and the presidency at a future date.

The name of the corporation was changed because it conflicted with companies in California and Michigan. Since we had two products under the "Novo" name, we changed the name of the company to Novo.

Sales were running about thirty-one million dollars a year in 1960. In 1960, we had a net loss of four hundred ninety-one thousand, five hundred fifty-nine dollars. We had a loss in 1961 of forty-two thousand, eight hundred seventy-seven, and a profit in 1962 of three hundred forty thousand, eight hundred. We hope for a half-million profit in 1963.

We cut our losses by old-fashioned cost-cutting, and unfortunately the bulk of this reduction had to be accomplished by elimination of excess overhead in the way of people. For the long pull, we began an active recruiting campaign for professional managers for most of the divisions. We now have six divisions and one subsidiary, after eliminating two of our divisions and replacing managers of four other divisions with professional managers. Of the four, two were incapable of adjusting their thinking to today's competitive business way of life. The other two were in their seventies, and were not effective managers.

As a general rule, I would say that the average business executive slows down in his seventies. As for the managers that we had to replace, they were not acclimated to running a competitive business. In fact, some of them did not even know the basic concepts of industrial management. They had been brought up in the boom years. Some of them did not want to change. There were some frustrating moments during the first couple of years, although the job was going to be done one way or the other. And some of the problems we found were a little deeper seated than appeared on the surface at first glance, and I'm still not completely satisfied with our progress. I don't think we've achieved the full measure of the company's long-range potential.

We have a long way to go, but Mr. Bronston has had some of the burden lifted from him. After all, Walter fathered Novo and put it together and it has certainly been very trying to him personally to have gone through the period of losses and the frustration of reorganization. I enjoy my position at Novo because I consider Walter the finest man I've ever met. He's sixty years old, about sixteen years older than myself, and we have a very compatible relationship. As for my personal progress, I can't say that I'm dissatisfied, but I still feel that I have a long way to go—I don't consider myself an old man. I didn't achieve what I set out to do twenty-five years ago quite as fast as I hoped, but by the same token there's always a little bit of optimism in any kind of projection.

The opportunities to succeed are even greater today because in the past ten years we've had an explosion in technology, in medicine, in business, and the economy is still changing. Because of this explosion I think there are more opportunities today, that's why if I had it to do all over again, I'd do pretty much what I have done, except I'd try to do it a little sooner, a little faster, and I would depend more on the wisdom of experienced people.

When a person is young he attempts to do so much on his own. He takes pride in figuring out his own problems, and he's reluctant to admit his ignorance. It's for this reason that one of the secrets of success, if you want to call it that, is by active participation. A young man gets valuable training in his early years sitting on a board of directors, working in fund-raising drives or service organizations.

A man in his early thirties is considered too young and inexperienced for a really big job. Unless he makes a breakthrough by his early forties then it's too late to start and he's considered too old. When you analyze this, it's a very, very short business-life span, so either you have to break it in that crucial period or else you're tabbed as a "has been" by the time you're in your fifties. And the only way to do that is by some kind of formal training. Believe me, an hour put into the trade associations, the Kiwanis, the Chamber of Commerce, are worth one hundred hours in return.

Also, you learn to motivate people—not manipulate them. The hardest thing for an executive to do is delegate work and authority; I think one of the highest forms of professional management is the ability to get a job done at the lowest possible echelon. This means you not only have to delegate, but the people you delegate to have to delegate, and right on through the second, third, and fourth levels, down to the sweeper or a man on the machine. *That* man has to do the job.

This is talent which can be developed by people with a limited education, but there's no question that not having a college degree is an obstacle today. You can overcome it to some extent, but it definitely is a disadvantage, and isn't something so taken for granted. For example, in Chicago I was invited to join a club because it was just assumed that I was a college grad. "Who's your alma mater?" they said. So I couldn't join, but I didn't have any intention of joining anyhow. I had already joined the Union League Club and saw no sense in joining another club.

But simply earning a degree isn't enough. Success is the yardstick that the individual sets up in his mind. I was a member of the parish of Father Charles Coughlin, the controversial "radio priest," and he said one day on the pulpit that men are not created equal. "Some of you fellows are going to be truck drivers, and all I can say is that if you are a truck driver, be a good one."

If a man is happy in his work—exerting himself to the full extent of his limitations and capabilities, and enjoying it—I'd say he's a success. And God help us if everyone in this world wanted to be a corporation president.

Basically, I've worked out a principle which I call the five per cent rule of thumb. I don't care in what field, whether it's Ford or a union organization, five per cent are leaders, ninety-five per cent are followers. I've applied that five per cent on a personal basis. If anyone does five per cent more than what they are supposed to, whether it's punching out on the job five minutes after five o'clock or coming in five minutes earlier, that formula breaks you from the follower to the leadership group. It can be applied in any organization.

Another point I want to mention: the president's job is one that, from my standpoint, requires sacrifice. He has to weigh his objectives to insure that both his family and outside interests get a fair shake. Personally, I've found that in my planning I can only do two basic things: be an executive and a combination father and husband. If you're raising a family, you're in partnership with your wife, and if you do a bum job in raising the children then you are a failure. You won't get a second chance to raise the kids.

One last thing I want to say. I'm very unhappy with the way the country is going. We seem to have lost the basic concept that this country was built on free enterprise in which business plays an important part. We now have a big government that seems to be growing upon itself and actually opposing the growth of free enterprise. Our government should be a driving force in fostering the very way of economic life which brought our government into being. The alternative is the Soviet state, but Washington seems more intent to fight U.S. business than the U.S.S.R. It may make sense politically, but it makes damned poor logic.

I see this situation worsening. The Federal alphabet bureaus are getting more and more power—power that surpasses the legislative and judicial departments. How can an F.C.C. Commissioner set the standards of what he thinks are proper radio standards to broadcast in the "public interest"? Who determines the public interest? A bureaucrat? If this trend is not arrested, if it continues uncontrolled, it could lose us our fight with the communistic world.

IX

*William G. Riley is a child of
our times in two respects: he managed to survive the
Depression and World War Two with no visible
scars. In five years his company, the Riley Management Corporation of Chicago, has survived its birth
pangs and gives every indication that it will thrive.*

WILLIAM G. RILEY

I make all my decisions based on one premise:
that the consumer must make a profit from what the seller
is selling, and he must make a greater profit than the
seller does. Now there has always been a lot of talk that
democracy and the free enterprise system is wonderful.
Many people say many times that Americanism is wonderful, communism is bad and socialism is bad, but not
enough say why. They say that we are the home of the
free and besides all of our political freedoms that we have,
we also are the best fed, the best clothed, the best housed,
the best vacationed, the best anything you want to talk
about, but there is not enough talk of why our system is
so successful. A lot of people always try to charge this off
to our natural resources, but it is a known fact that South

America has more minerals in the ground than we have, and that there are portions of Asia that are much more fertile than our country. So it isn't our natural resources. We were once an underdeveloped country, and now the underdeveloped countries want to understand how we did it.

It's very simple. We have a system that works on the weakness of man. Man does not do anything for his fellow man. If my grass needs cutting, I'm certainly not going to cut your grass. If my kids are going hungry, I'm not going to feed your kids. But I will cut your grass, or feed your kids, if my grass is already cut and my kids are already fed. Then I'll give you some of my surplus. But this is philanthropy. Being a philanthropist is giving away some of your surplus. But you will never give away what you need. I doubt very much that our great men did what they did for mankind. Fulton certainly didn't develop the steamboat for his fellow man, because his fellow man ridiculed him while he was building his boat.

The man who discovered fire was probably burned at the stake for his troubles. So, man does things more for himself than for humanity. Now in our country and in our system, in order to take care of yourself, you have to take care of your fellow man. By this I mean that any product which is successful in this country, the buyer makes the greatest profit. Let's take a General Motors refrigerator, for example. Let's say after they sell it, their profit is fifteen dollars. And let's say you begrudge them their fifteen dollars and decide you're going to do without a refrigerator. Now the extra trips you have to make to the store, the food that goes bad, the inconvenience would add up to far more than fifteen dollars. Let's say you wanted to make a refrigerator equivalent to G.M.'s in your basement. This might cost you a hundred thousand dollars. So, when you buy their refrigerator, you make a much greater profit than they do.

The way I like best to illustrate this is with a can of peas. Del Monte makes peas and they sell them for, let's say, eighteen cents. They make a tenth of a cent profit. Now Del Monte never cares whether you eat another pea for the rest of your life. The only reason they are making peas is for the profit involved in the peas. Let's say you're a bricklayer making four-fifty an hour, which is a good wage. You can begrudge Del Monte that tenth of a cent profit on the can of peas by growing your own peas, canning them, and the whole thing might cost you two hours or run you about eight eighty-two more than buying them from Del Monte. Now this goes for absolutely any product you look at. Just merely sit down and analyze how you would do it if you never bought the product in the first place and you'll find that the consumer is making a thousand times what the seller is making. There are only three exceptions to this: booze, gambling, and vices, and these are known as items of exploitation. With everything else, the consumer makes much more than the seller.

It's the buyer who's the guy making the big profit. In order to successfully merchandise a product, to get the thing started, you've got to say that if somebody doesn't buy my product, they are worse off than I am. But they would be better off if they bought my product. And when you've got that ingredient, you've got a successful product which can be merchandised. In other words, to create a successful product, you must help your fellow man, even though your motive is selfish. I have been asked if people are ever exploited even if they benefit from the product. This can only happen if there is not an open market.

I happen to sell apartments. I cannot tell you that my King Arthur Apartments are nice apartments, or beautiful apartments. I can't say, "Isn't this kitchen gorgeous?" It means nothing. I've got to point out that my kitchen is better than all the other kitchens on the market. I've got to say that isn't this reasonable rent compared to other rent. None of us really know what anything is worth. Quality is only relative to other products. Price is only relative to other products. Now when you lose the relative comparison, you no longer have anything. This is why, when I am training a salesman, I push him to make everything relative to something, or they have said nothing. It just has to be by comparison. The wide open market is our safety valve against exploitation.

I build a better-than-average apartment. I think I build the best apartment in the area. I'm able to beat my chest and say my apartments are the best, but if I didn't have competition, I couldn't say this. My apartments are the best only compared to what other people are building. I always make the point around here that we are not too sharp, it's that our competition is too dull. And, if we are good, we are only good by comparison to the others. But let's sit down and analyze ourselves singularly. Let's not bring our competition into our own comparison, and we find out that we have a lot of shortcomings. We have a lot of ways we have to improve ourselves. We have a lot of ways we have to grow, and sometimes we seek success or take credit for success just too easily, because our competition is not forcing us to be as good as we should be.

There are different badges of success. Part of success is

making money, yet when you make substantial money, you soon realize that it isn't all-important. If you have been raised a certain way, you can only spend so much money. Now there are exceptions that have come along in this life—screwballs, and they throw money all over the place, but thank goodness, they are exceptions. Now let's say that you could easily afford a quart of milk, but I don't think you would go to the sink and pour a quart of milk down the drain. Not that you couldn't afford the quarter the quart of milk costs, but it's just that I don't think you enjoy sheer waste. Most of us cannot spend real big money because we feel it is sheer waste. This is what I say is spending big money. You go out and buy a yacht for one hundred thousand dollars. You find a mooring spot on Lake Michigan which costs a thousand a month. You hire a captain for ten thousand a year and three deck hands for six thousand a year—and then you use that yacht one Saturday all summer. Now this is to spend big money. But to be able to do this, you have to be raised with money and most of us are not that fortunate. Now we had a maid for about a year. I finally told my wife, "I just don't enjoy living in a house with a maid in it." I could easily afford the maid, but we found ourselves ill-at-ease so consequently we no longer have a maid. The rich will have a home in Palm Beach which they haven't seen in two years, and a home on the Riviera that they haven't seen for three years, but these people can do it only because they are used to such luxuries.

I have discovered that I cannot spend more than five hundred dollars a week. I'm quite sure that if I were to make more than a million dollars a year, my personal spending power could never exceed five hundred dollars a week. As it is, when I spend five hundred dollars a week, I'm wasting a great deal of money. I'm not shopping around for bargains and I'm not really paying too much attention to prices. I still take my vacations and I drive the best automobile. I live in more home than I need, in a fine neighborhood. And yet, I am not exceeding five hundred dollars a week. A house with fifteen bedrooms and six servants would have no purpose to me. What I am trying to say is that after a certain point, increased earnings will not raise your standard of living.

Yet making money, even though you don't use it personally, is still a badge of success. When you're on a relay team in school, or on a debating team, you fight for the cup or the medal. When you finally get this gold pin that says you came in first, you can't cash it in for anything but you take great pride in the fact that you've won the pin. Making money, in the same way, is one of the badges of success. It means that you have been successful and that you made your success correctly and honestly and that you've won. And so, how do you know if a fellow's a successful businessman? If he's worth money.

I was raised during the Depression and that's where I've developed this inability to live on more than five hundred dollars a week. I was born in Cleveland, Ohio, but we left there when I was eighteen months old, so naturally I know nothing about Cleveland. We moved to Westchester, New York, but by 1934 the Depression caught up with my father and we moved to Brooklyn. I didn't realize then that anything was abnormal. I thought it was just ordinary and common to do without. As a family, we had our rough periods but so did everyone else. When I look back, I now realize that all the families were more closely knit than they are today because everybody worked for the common interest. That common interest was survival.

When you went out and got a job as a kid, it wasn't so that you could buy a baseball or get some ice skates or put two dollars in your piggy bank or something like that. If you earned any money, it went into that common pot and it created food on the table, and this meant that you lived for another two weeks longer. I can't remember not ever having a job. I worked after school and Saturdays and Sundays and holidays and any available time to have a job. The money I made was a considerable aid to the family. Maneuvering around, I could go out and make ten dollars a week. This ten dollars not only bought a great deal more, it also was ten dollars that had not been available. Today, we look at gaining money as only a matter of being willing to sacrifice to gain money. You're willing to work, you want to take a second job, or you want to pump gas on the weekends. As long as you want to do something, then you have the ingredient to make some money. All you have to be is willing to devote your time and in turn you will get money for this willingness.

During the Depression, you could have been willing to work for twenty-five cents an hour and you could have been willing to work anytime, anywhere, doing anything, but still there wasn't anything available for you to do. So, then, the significant point was not how much you made, but that you made anything at all.

My dad was a sharp man. He was extremely bright and

he wasn't lazy, but his talents were executive—and who needed executives? He came back slightly a couple of times, only to stumble again. In 1941, he came back real strong and did all right for himself from then on, but during the Depression, he was one of the boys who caught it. My sister was an excellent student. She was always very high in her class, and when it came time for her to go to college, we couldn't think of sending her to college. The money just wasn't there to send her.

The big difference I find today from the Depression years is that today there is shame if you're poor or you're not able to afford something or not able to do something. Then, there was no shame in being poor. Everybody was, and it wasn't exactly embarrassing if you had the lights turned off or the landlord was knocking at your door. It was just bad luck and bad conditions. Today, if you put a kid to work, people say, "Wouldn't it be good if he had this job during the summer?" or, "Wouldn't it be wonderful if he had a newspaper route?" or they say, "It's good training." We had all of those jobs—we had the newspaper routes; we had the jobs of delivering the groceries. But the last intention that our families ever had was that we had those jobs for training or the "development of a good background." We worked because our families needed the money, and everybody was counted on to help.

As a kid, I never received any kind of an allowance. If I made a few dollars, I could hold back ten or fifteen cents but never did they give us any money. I don't think any kid ever got any money. Today, kids go on strike if you don't give them enough. For a while I lived across the street from Brooklyn College and for years over there I was the Number One magazine salesman. When I was nine, ten, and eleven years old, I was making nearly five dollars a week selling magazines. My family made one rule: I could never sell to anyone we knew, or to anyone in the building, or any relative. I always had to sell as a stranger.

I worked in a kosher butcher shop, and I ran a mangle in a laundry for a while. At one time in my life, an uncle had given me one of those lead soldiers kits. You poured hot lead into the mold and when you opened it up, you had a lead soldier. And I discovered that a lot of kids in the neighborhood would want to buy the soldiers. The problem was to get lead. I discovered that in New York City, whenever Con Edison was doing any kind of repair work, there was always scrap lead left over from the job. I went up to some of the men and asked them for some lead and naturally they turned me down. I tried to figure out a way to get them obligated to me. I discovered that they were always in need of a cold glass of water.

So, I'd start off the day with a pitcher, and I would knock on somebody's door and ask if I could have some ice. Naturally, they would give me some ice without too much trouble. I'd go over to a spigot on the outside of a house and I'd fill this pitcher with water, and all day long I would stand there and keep those men working on the job supplied with ice water. At the end of the day, I'd ask if there was any extra lead, and they used to weight me down with the stuff. I mean, I don't imagine Con Edison was so crazy about it, but I got a hell of a lot of lead. Then I'd go and make lead soldiers by the hundreds.

Where I lived in Brooklyn, there was a subway junction

nearby at the end of the line where an awful lot of people came out every day. I started selling lead soldiers at this street corner for a penny apiece, or six for a nickel. Every Friday or Saturday, I'd sell three or four hundred lead soldiers. On a good Friday or Saturday, I could make five or six dollars. The people who bought the soldiers from me didn't buy them simply to give a kid some business. They were poor, too. They were looking for some kind of a gift they could bring home to their kid, and for two cents they could pick up two soldiers. At the end of the year, the kid would have fifty or a hundred soldiers and I would have fifty cents or a dollar. I worked at this for five or six years, and did real well with it and probably made hundreds and hundreds of dollars doing it.

In 1941, my dad came out of the Depression. He was a Wall Street man and when the market started to move, he started to make some money. He rented a place up near Greenwich, Connecticut, and it was the first good living accommodations that we had had in years. By this time, my sister had joined the SPARS and there were only three of us.

I had been having a number of difficulties at school. I was not the best behaved student. It was a pretty rough neighborhood that I was brought up in, and I don't think any of the kids I knew were doing that well in school. When my father was financially able, he sent me away to a military school but that lasted only until I went into the service. I enlisted on my seventeenth birthday and went in during the middle of 1943. I became a signalman in the Navy and went through a few invasions out in the South Pacific and came back home.

I actually feel that the war was the biggest break I could have had since I had absolutely no education to speak of. I had no high school diploma. I had taken a number of correspondence courses while in the Navy with the New York Institute of Finance and had become pretty familiarized with various financial statements and the mechanics of the securities business. When I got out of the service, I found that the only requirement needed to get a job was to be a veteran. They really didn't care whether you had one year of high school or four years of college, and they hired people accordingly. I believe that today no kid would get the same opportunity. I was nineteen when I got out of the service. Today, a kid of nineteen is still a kid. But then, at nineteen, I wasn't looked at as a kid because I had been away to war and they gave me opportunities that not everyone would get today. I went to work for a brokerage house and started trading securities.

That brokerage firm traded the stock of the Indiana Limestone Company. One day, some officials of Indiana Limestone came East and said they were looking for some young blood and thought it would be good to get a couple of New Yorkers in there. They offered me a job and I accepted. It looked like a chance for improvement and I moved to Bedford, Indiana, where I stayed for two years. In the course of training me, they sent me out to look at a mill in Bloomington. They asked me to take a look at it and give them a report.

I thought the mill was run terribly. They had no efficiency whatsoever and, because of my detailed report, the company ended up by putting me in charge of the mill. At the time, the mill was turning out only about fifteen thousand cubic feet of stone a month and had lost money for a good many years. Within six months, I had pushed the mill up to one hundred thousand cubic feet a month. I rapidly moved up to where I was making about a thousand dollars a month with the company and, in about a year and a half, I was about fourth in command in the company. Then I got in the middle of a proxy fight. Since I was more in favor of the people who were in than the people who were coming in, I got out of there.

I thought I could do a lot better as a mason contractor, so I started into contracting with a traveling gang. I worked in Gary, Cincinnati, Dayton, Chicago, Philadelphia, and Birmingham. Finally the traveling got too rough, so I looked around for an area to settle in and do contracting. I chose Chicago. In traveling around the country, I noticed that the Midwesterner seemed only to be concerned about how quick he can get a job done, how much it will cost, and what the terms are, and it was possible to make a deal with a Midwesterner the first time you called on him. In New York, though, if you're trying to sell a product, the New Yorker listens to what you have to say and, after you leave, he sees if he can get it wholesale, or whether his brother-in-law can sell it to him. Then, after you make a deal with somebody in New York, they're always shooting around to see whether they can make a better deal. In New England, you're not going to sell anyone until you've called on them eight or nine times. In the South, I discovered they don't like to do business with anyone but Southerners, and when a Damn Yankee comes in there to sell, they're leery of him and they don't trust him. On the West Coast, I've found that you can never rest on your laurels. They're always looking for something bigger and better with a crazy gimmick. So I chose Chicago. I didn't have one friend in the town and I didn't have one business contact.

The first thing I tried to do was to import those Hoosiers up to Chicago to work stone for me, but I discovered they would rather starve in Indiana than make money in Chicago. After a while, I realized that stonework alone was hard to come by in Chicago, so I figured I would have to learn the brick laying end of it. I disbanded stone contracting, went out and got myself a job as a laborer with a brick gang, and worked real hard to get the chance to lay brick. I got my chance and because of my stone experience, I was soon a qualified union bricklayer, making two ninety-five an hour. I don't think people who haven't done it realize what hard work construction laboring is.

Eventually I had my own bricklaying gang and I probably could have gone through life making between fifteen and thirty thousand dollars a year at it if I had been satisfied. One thing became a fact: you couldn't make money over the winter and consequently you were better off to be idle from about Thanksgiving Day to St. Patrick's Day.

One winter when I was wondering what the hell to do, a friend informed me that he had some six-flats out in Glen Ellyn that were empty and we made a deal for me to try to rent and sell them.

That first year selling, without having any experience, I made one hundred thousand dollars. I never had this kind of financial success before. Then, I realized that I could more than make a living at it. I must admit that at the time I did not enjoy my work as much as I enjoyed laying brick—even though I was making one hundred thousand a year. Now, I've gotten used to real estate and I am now busy enough so that I enjoy what I am doing now more than laying brick.

I knew real quickly that the builders were not putting up the right kind of apartments, although the apartments they were building were being rented and were making money for the owners. I could see that people were taking these apartments as a second choice and the reason they were successful was that there was nothing better on the market. I also could see that there was a larger market for one-bedrooms than in any other market. And I could see that apartment renters and house renters were really divided into two categories—people without children preferred to live in apartments and people with children wanted to live in houses. You could see this division and could start to formulate on how to go after what category of people and what was possible.

And right then I decided to build apartment developments, all with one-bedroom apartments. Now I was anxious as hell to go into building. I would have loved to become a general contractor at the time and start building. But I saw that the builders were doing plenty of building but hadn't any merchandising methods to take care of their apartments. I figured that I'll first of all build a method to sell mousetraps and then I'll build a better mousetrap. I marked time and spent nearly two years building a renting and management organization. All my employees became specialized in the ability to rent apartments.

I became the largest rental office on the west side of

Chicago. I had dozens of people working for us and several offices, and all the time I was building this machine to rent apartments. When I felt that I had a good enough renting organization, I started my developments. I figured there was plenty of investment money around and all I did was put a lot of ads in the Chicago papers which appealed to what I called "armchair investors"—that is, professional men and people with money to invest who didn't want the headaches of managing an apartment. I got plenty of takers. I promised the investors a twelve per cent return on their money and full occupancy of the apartment for at least a year. The way it's turned out, my first development has been open for more than two years and we don't have a single vacancy.

I looked around for some exciting land and I found a lovely tract in Addison, Illinois. There were a few shacks on the land but I got rid of them. And there was a creek that ran through the land but had gotten polluted. I cleaned up the creek and built a two-hundred-four-unit development. It's an absolute beauty. There's a swimming pool, a pitch and put golf course, canoes on the creek, tennis courts, barbecue pits, and the whole works. I would only build a building after I had sold it so there was nothing speculative about the thing. The people flocked to it. We've never had a vacancy there.

I'm now finishing up a seven-hundred-seventy-six-unit development in Northlake, Illinois, and I haven't had a bit of trouble renting the apartments. My investors are doing wonderfully. They're making twelve per cent on their cash investment and I'd say they're making about thirty-five per cent on their money in property gain. My smallest investor buys a share in one of my developments for twenty-eight thousand dollars. I don't accept anything smaller. Most of the investors put in larger amounts. My biggest problem is finding the right piece of land and getting the zoning for it. If I could hurdle that problem then I could sell ten times as much as I'm selling right now. But the trouble is you've got a lunacy element that appears in most small towns, and this element will fight you no matter what you plan for that town. If you go into a town and you tell the town fathers that you want to build a house for crippled children and you'll operate it for free, why I guarantee you one hundred people will march on City Hall saying we don't want any cripples in our town. I don't care what you go to do, you've got the "againsters" and the people who are against go to every meeting. The people who are for never go to a meeting.

My Northlake project will run, when completed, around ten million dollars. I've got another development of six thousand starting in Westmont. Also in the works is a fifteen-million-dollar King Arthur and one going on the Fox River that will be about four million dollars, and still another one on the west side of town that will cost about five million dollars.

Naturally, the bigger a development is the more money it represents. The capacity of the area determines on how big they will be. You can never fill the needs of an area. If you completely fill the needs of the area, then you have no waiting lists. If the market was good for two thousand of my apartments, I'd never build more than one thousand. If the area was good for seven thousand, I might build four thousand. But I would never completely fill the need.

I'd always want that not everyone can rent or buy our buildings. One of the greatest sales aids we have is that when you come around to buying a building in Northlake or Addison you can't have one, they're all sold. This makes people want them just that much more.

I formed my company in 1958. Presently, it's doing about a million dollars' worth of business a month. Last year, we made about half a million in profit; this year we'll probably do twice as good. You have to understand in a new company you are forced to reinvest your profits right back into expansion and land purchases, so consequently it's still a struggle.

My wife and myself own ninety-five per cent of the company. My attorney owns the other five per cent. Although I consider my wife and I partners I do not have an arrangement where I would need her signature. I've seen too many men tied up in a bundle needing their wife's signature, and while I'm head of this ship, I'm not going to let that happen to me. What happens if I have a fight with my wife at the breakfast table in the morning and I have to sign a deal with her in the afternoon? My wife is well protected by other means. I think a big mistake a lot of men make in a corporation is that when they form it, they automatically make their wife secretary-treasurer. I say make your wife the vice-president and make your attorney the secretary-treasurer and stop needing that signature.

When I go out to my two developments, I'm the happiest I've ever been. People keep coming up and complimenting you on how nice their apartments are. I think this is wonderful. It's great. We all like these personal pats on the back, and I like them as much as anyone else. I think that the biggest kick there is if you can sit down and say the world is better off because I'm alive, because I am here, and when it comes time to turn in your ticket, you can say that you have done a good thing or two.

I would like to take my King Arthur apartments nationally, all across the country. I would like it to be a brand name. I would like to say I have created a brand name. I think I'll make it nationally. The reason I'm convinced is that I believe we have the right answers and enjoy our work.

I am fearful at times of becoming an old conservative fogey as I grow older. I have tried to be very aware of this thing. It is progressive thinking that becomes so opinionated that they don't realize that time and conditions have changed, so in turn become outdated. One must realize that a continuous state of happiness is not physically possible. After all, if you never experience unhappiness, how would you know you were happy? Being happy is only a relative state of being. Let's use a steak to illustrate my point. If all you ever ate was a good steak how would you know it was good? Only by eating a bad steak could you learn to appreciate a good steak. The same thing with happiness.

At times an unhappy state just seems to settle in with no real reason. But having some goal we have yet to obtain gives us the needed excuse to get by this depressed period, such as, if I got a raise I would be happy or I need a boat to be happy, and so forth. Of course, the problem lies in that if all your goals are obtained you lose this needed excuse. A lofty goal such as world peace is what we all need. In other words, easily obtainable trashy goals will not bring happiness.

X

John H. Ballard is practically a textbook example of the poor boy who made good. He worked for the Bulova Watch Company for fifty years, rising from office boy to president. But when he reached the age of sixty-five, he run into a problem that Horatio Alger never had: enforced retirement. He did not take to retirement with ease, and now he is the president of a Bulova competitor, the Gruen Watch Company.

JOHN H. BALLARD

In 1909, I went to work for the Bulova Company for four dollars a week. I came from South Brooklyn, and my father and his father were in the building line; they were mechanics, all mechanics. The whole family was mechanics. I was helping my father and somehow or other I didn't like that work. It was dirty, or something like that, you know. So I walked down Broadway, went to an employment agency at 170 Broadway and they sent me over to Bulova, who was at 51 Maiden Lane, and I got a position there at four dollars a week.

At the time I had very good handwriting and I guess Ardie Bulova liked the way I wrote my name down. And I got the job. So I quit high school. My mother wanted me to continue to go to school, and I just wanted to go to work, so I went to work, that's all. You got to work at about five minutes to eight and you had to clean out the office a little. Brush it out. The office consisted of Emily Bulova Henschel, Ardie Bulova, who was selling, and in the back was the factory with Joseph Bulova running it. Joseph was Ardie's father and the founder of the company. He was a wonderful man, kindly, fatherly, always encouraging you and always the first in the door in the morning. I left around five-thirty and went to the post office to mail some little packages and things like that, and then I went home. I left my house at a quarter to seven in the morning and got home, on an average, at a quarter past seven.

After I was there for a few months I got a raise to five dollars a week. It was because I knew a little something about bookkeeping. I could help in those days with the single-entry books. And there was the bank book to be balanced, you know, and the petty cash and things like that. We were in the jewelry business then, not the watch business, making cufflinks, bracelets, and so forth.

When I was there about seven or eight months, I used to sell a little goods over the counter. On my way home to Brooklyn, I would put a few samples in my pocket and I got five per cent to sell some goods, on some goods a little more. And sometimes I could make two or three dollars a week that way. I would sell to jewelers all along Brooklyn, and I got a little commission on that. I guess I was about seventeen when I first started to sell.

I didn't get nervous or anything like that. That doesn't bother me at all. I always found in selling, don't talk too much. You see, just go in and kind of go easy about it. Let the other fellow talk because if he talks you'll always know what is in his mind and you have his mind and your mind and therefore you know what to do.

I think that most salesmen talk too much. They don't give the buyer a chance to come out with what he wants to ask in questions. And then in selling you should never use all your selling opportunities fast and have nothing left. Keep things in the back of your mind as you go along and the man is in the process of buying.

Sometime around 1914 we decided to go into the watch business. Women in the U.S. had been wearing chatelaine watches on a pin, but the women in Europe were wearing them on the wrist. So we started making a few watches for the wrist and it built up pretty good and it kept going along. Then we started making a line, and we got an idea for boxing the watches and using certain names on the watch outside of the name of Bulova—like Maxim and Rubaiyat and things like that. Gradually, I was getting in charge of the sales force because I was there the longest. I used to help breaking in salesmen throughout the country. I was about twenty-six years old at the time when I was sales manager.

Eventually Bulova grew very, very big. We worked hard, made the right products and then we started to do national advertising. And we went along and one of the good things that I think helped us was that we went on radio—that was one of the jobs I had. I got more into the marketing and then I used to watch advertising and selling and things like that. One day I figured that it might make sense to buy spot announcements on radio to give people the time of day and things like news and weather. It wasn't easy to buy a spot announcement from a station after a certain hour, but I was able to do it. We figured a system of chimes, which I originated, and then the announcer would say, "It's eleven o'clock, B-U-L-O-V-A, Bulova Watch Time." I think that this was one of the biggest things that helped Bulova come along and grow.

Then we got into credit selling. Many jewelers were cash stores but I converted them into credit jewelers. We started with credit selling in Baltimore and in Detroit and then we expanded that. Got more jewelers to go into it— and they have all made very, very good money. Opened up chain stores and all. We learned very quickly more people will buy if they can buy a watch on time with a small payment down and pay for it as they wear it—the same as an automobile. If you were to sell automobiles so that everybody had to pay cash, you wouldn't sell as many and you would not sell as many watches. And by doing that, of course, you create more employment for Americans. And you know most things are sold that way today.

Some of the biggest chains in the country with hundreds of stores all started in one credit store here and there. What we were doing then was pioneering the watch business: we were packaging the watch, pricing a watch, merchandising the watch, and all the time converting an industry from a cash approach to one where the market is expanded fifty to one hundred times through credit selling. Things were going so good that one year, when I was still less than forty years old, I was getting a percentage of the increase in sales and I was making at least fifty-five thousand dollars a year. In 1935, when I was forty-two, I was made president of Bulova. I'd been there for about twenty-six years. But even though I was president, things were just the way they'd always been at Bulova—it was really a two-man team: I took care of the marketing, which included selling, the merchandising and the advertising; and Ardie Bulova, who was one of the finest manufacturers I knew, ran all of the factories throughout the country and the world and took care of the financial end of it.

Then I'll tell you what happened. All of a sudden I found myself at the age of sixty-five. Well, at sixty-five you are supposed to retire. Ardie Bulova had passed away, and I stayed on one year longer. And at the end of that year I was still a director, of course. Well, they went ahead and elected a new president. I had a very large pension— if you want to know how much, it was over forty thousand dollars a year. And I was still on the board of directors, but it was a very peculiar situation. A lot of times new people when they go to running a business never want to ask an old-timer any questions or how we did this or how we would solve that. The new president was a nephew of Ardie Bulova. So, they didn't seem to want me to stay around any longer than the extra year that I had already stayed, so I cleaned out my files and left. Actually, it took a good two months to get all of the things straightened out and then suddenly I was finished after working for the company for fifty years.

It's a funny thing, you keep working not really thinking about retirement and then all of a sudden it hits you. In looking back on my retirement I think the biggest mistakes that all firms make is that they don't plan to break in anyone to become a president when the old president is getting ready to retire. Sometimes some people think they know different things and if they don't use somebody's talents, well, that is up to them. You want to know my feelings? Well, I'll tell you. You don't feel very good when you leave all your friends and people you worked with, a lot of them who you built up to big positions and things like that. Nobody can feel good about that.

That last day after cleaning up everything I went downstairs and all of the help gave me a nice party. They had a few dances and drinks and so on and then I left. And so I didn't do anything and you get retired and you sit home and the first day you don't know what to do with yourself.

I'll tell you truthfully about that first day when you don't have to go to work. You get up, you hang around and read the paper—you get up at seven o'clock anyway. You stall around, you know, so you don't know what to do with yourself and you don't want to stay around the house. You take a walk. You have lunch. You walk past the Plaza movie house on Fifty-eighth Street and, for the first time in my life in the middle of the week, I went to a movie. I think it was "The Apartment."

The next day I just stalled around some more and the next day was the same as the previous day except I had lunch with some friends and then went over and got a massage at Reilly's. Then maybe I'd go over to 630 Fifth Avenue, where I had a small office, and stop for a lot of personal mail that I get, all to do with stocks and so forth. And you go to the bank and you walk. Boy, do you walk! Meantime, some people were after me to go to work for them—especially the Gruen people—but I just hadn't made up my mind yet. And then another day I walked up Park Avenue and I looked at all of the foreign cars. I'd stop into the Waldorf, and I smoke a cigar and I probably have a sandwich or something—and I'll tell you I roamed around until I was nuts. One day I had to get out of the house because that is the day they do the house cleaning and, boy, do you get swept out! So I went around. I still had a lot of personal business to do. You have investments and bills to pay and so forth. And that would take about an hour a day, you know what I mean? And there were so many people I wanted to see for lunch and this and that and so forth. And then I'm a director of several corporations—Standard Finance Company and such—and that would kill some time, too.

It's pretty funny about your friends when you retire. What I mean is, you see quickly who are your friends and who are acquaintances. Friends are all right, but people who were using you, well, you know that saying: "What did you do for me lately?" You know that story? Well, that's it. You see a lot of people who you thought were your friends but they are not your friends. And you will find that out all of the time.

I don't want to name any names, but those people are around. Some people you have done marvelous things for and made them, and then when you're out they don't even want to know you. In fact, there are some people that I haven't heard one word from since I have been over at Gruen. You never hear a word. But there are some real friends who always call you up, come and visit you and so forth. You find out after you are not the president any more that a lot of people don't even want to know you because you can't do anything for them. They don't even bother. They may say hello to you.

But I'm used to it. It doesn't bother me. Those things don't bother you. You've got to take them. You know, Ardie Bulova always said that I knew one thing: I knew how to analyze a man. And I know those who are phonies, and those who aren't phonies. Truthfully, whether people were phonies or not didn't make any difference to me. As long as they did their job right.

Well, finally, after about three weeks of going absolutely nuts I decided to go to Gruen. That was in the fall of 1959. Gruen had been losing money for eight years, something like eleven million dollars. But some new money was put into the company. I knew the investors. I was told that the inventory was worth so much. I was told that they had orders of so much. But to my great surprise I found that the orders they had booked were no good, and that the inventory was worth, well, I'd say about fifty per cent of what it had been estimated to me.

Plain and simple, the people who had talked me into coming in had given me a very, very optimistic picture. In order to get me, they painted the picture as brightly as possible. That first year I cut the losses from a million eight hundred thousand dollars to five hundred nine thousand dollars. In 1962, the company showed a small profit— $118,000—the first time they'd showed a profit in eight years. And things look even better in 1963. It will be well up into six figures.

Believe you me, it wasn't easy. I got in usually around nine o'clock, and a lot of times I had to wait out in the hall until somebody opened the door. Finally, I said, "How do we work here?" People were coming in at all hours. And they said, "We have an honor system." That was some honor system! Nobody knew who went to lunch or when they came back or anything like that. People were coming in at nine-thirty and ten o'clock, working late, getting overtime for their working late. The money was dribbling out in that direction. We were paying half again for a job which should have been done within the regular time.

As a matter of fact, nine-thirty was early. They'd usually straggle in at ten just in time for Schrafft's, which would come around and serve coffee and rolls and so forth. At lunch time they would go out for a couple of hours to do their shopping. And then around three o'clock they all went down on what was supposed to be their second coffee break to Schrafft's for lunch. Then they were all busy. And of course they had to work overtime. It was the internal situation of the company which had to be re-molded completely from top to bottom. You had to start from scratch.

Well, I stopped all that. I had to put off the honor system and put in a clock to be punched and the people would work their regular time, which I know is less than forty hours, and they still got time off for coffee breaks. Sometimes people would say to me, "At your age, what are you fooling around here? . . ." And I was trying to say, "Well, maybe I am the Casey Stengel of the watch industry." Because Stengel started something like I did in his new position. And he went through the first year what I had to go through. And he done it because he loved baseball, and probably I did because I loved the watch business.

Those things that I did were on the personnel side. But

to save a company on the business side, first of all you have to have years of experience in the watch business. You know your trade. And you have to work hard. Be in every day. You had to line and control your inventory. And you had to start getting rid of your old inventory. Watch movements can be salvaged. Maybe the dial was poor. So you redial it. It costs you a couple of dollars but you sell it, not at a big profit. Then you have a lot of merchandise around that cost too much or was getting a little out of style. Anyhow, you get rid of all of that. Maybe I'd take a watch and put a very beautiful bracelet on it. The bracelet might cost more than the average one, but you're better off because at least you're able to sell the watch, even if you make a dollar or two less than you would have.

And then I'd stand there every two weeks and go through the book of every watch that was sold and stick with getting rid of the numbers you are not going to run any more. And I want to tell you they called me every kind of pest in the world, but I got that list, and I knew every week how many of each kind were sold. And that's the way I broke down that inventory. And when you got that broke down, you know you're on your way.

Anyhow, I loved working again. Even with all of the headaches, I liked it. But I want to tell you, it was pretty rough. I was working harder than I ever was before. The hours don't mean anything. It's just how many hours you really work. I'm not one to go out. I go downstairs and take fifteen minutes and get lunch. I'm on the job in the morning and I line up my goods and toward the end of the afternoon I probably don't have too much to do. But the hours don't mean anything. I think that anybody who has to work a lot of overtime, well, I think the boss ought to find out why. Either he don't have enough help or he don't know how to do anything fast enough. And then he needs someone to take his place. I don't believe in these people who have to stay overtime to do certain things. There's no need for it.

As for the jewelers who did business with us, well, they didn't flock in, in the beginning. You don't blame them because they weren't buying at Gruen. They just didn't know what would happen to the company. One of my good friends who has a chain of stores did come in and he said he wanted to pick out a complimentary order of one hundred watches. "I don't care what they are," he said. Instead of taking charity, we sat down and we gave them a good promotion pitch to sell Gruen. And that was in November and the promotion ran for three weeks. Instead of buying one hundred watches from us he bought twenty-five thousand dollars' worth of watches and sold them all. We gave him a good promotion. And that's what you've got to do. When you're selling somebody, you've got to give them reasons to know how he can also sell it. You've got to have some ideas. And eventually all of the big jewelry chains came in here, friends of mine.

Not many people know this, but I had to give up that forty-thousand-dollar-a-year pension from Bulova to go to Gruen. You see, the arrangement was I was to get forty-thousand-a-year pension if I didn't go to work for another watch company, but if I did I automatically forfeited the pension. I found it very easy to drop that pension but a lot of people don't. They retire and they sit home and they don't have enough to do and sometimes they don't live too long. Their mind gets blank. They sit home with the television. Their body doesn't circulate right and before you know it they seem to pass away. I think it is an insurance to life to work, to work a little longer. It keeps yourself going. As for me, I didn't bother my family hanging around the house those three weeks I was home. They'd keep going one place or another. I had children late in life and they are out to school, so I wasn't in their way.

But I'm an exception. People are living longer and all of those pension forms were never figured out by a lot of people until they retired. I don't know what we're going to do with people who've got a good brain when they get to a certain age. That's going to be one of our biggest problems in the next decade. And if we let those who are getting older stay around, what about the younger men who want to move up? If the old people don't move out how can the young people move up? I think this is a big problem, and it's got to be done gradually. It is terrible to have a man working hard until the day he retires and all of a sudden he retires and he doesn't have anything to do.

I think a year or two before a man is supposed to retire he should be given an extra week or two of vacation so he'll get some idea of what it's like to be doing nothing. Or maybe companies could make a rule whereby these fellows should come down to the office at ten o'clock in the morning and leave at four. Also, these older fellows should gradually break in the younger fellows and be honest enough to teach the youngsters everything they know. And then probably he should be a consultant to the company for a couple of years, maybe take a vacation here and there, and sort of work his way out gradually getting into some hobby or something else to do.

There is no law that says you can't keep working. The only law in the United States is that you can collect your Social Security at the age of sixty-two if you're not working. The whole thing should be gradual with the older man working his way out and the younger man working his way up. Maybe an old idea and a young idea works out pretty well for a company.

Trouble is, from most of the young people I've seen they're already counting their pension, forgetting they got thirty-five or forty years of work ahead of them. Most young people, it seems to me, are in a rut. They would like to get to where they make so much a week and they can't wait until their pensions so they don't have anything to do. Those sort of people are just ordinary employees in a place. They don't have enough drive. They work for all kind of companies. They all tell you, "When I get to be so many years old and I get so much money a week, I'm going to move to Florida or to California and I'll live there and really enjoy life." They just want to take it easy. I'll tell you plain—they're lazy.

We have kids who come up to Gruen for jobs, twenty-three and twenty-four years old, and the first question they ask is, "Do you have a pension plan?" And I spoke with a few of them and I am amazed. What are they worrying about forty years from now? It seems that the same drives aren't present today that were present a generation ago. They all want to know when they join a firm if when they get to a certain age will they have enough money to live on. That's all. And some of them work for firms and become bookkeepers, clerks, and that is all they will ever be. And the companies themselves help foster this by having pension plans, so I don't know what the solution is.

I just don't understand why young people are afraid of taking a chance. When I was a kid, a friend of mine who was an attorney sent me over to the New York Central Rail Road there to be interviewed for a job. So I went over there—I was working for Bulova for a short while by then—and I saw all of those people at their desks and one man at a high desk, like a teacher. I told him what I was doing at Bulova. He said, "Well, you can come right to work here. I don't know how many years it will take you to get from down there to up where I am, but come on and work for us." I ran out of there.

If I was starting out today I'd pick a good large company and I would want to be damn sure that the heads of it were hard workers and would have brains. And there's plenty of companies I know of that have come up fast in the last ten years. Is there anything wrong with someone who started with Revlon? They started with just that lip-stick. Is there anything wrong with somebody who went with Korvette? They started with just one store.

If people are going to go to college, I believe that any-one who goes to college should go to college for a reason. If they are going to college to be a lawyer, a doctor, a writer, or advertising—fine, let them study that. And you should go to college with the idea of studying that one subject there so that when you come out you'll know some-thing and can go to a firm and do something along the lines you studied. The most important thing is to do something that you like. If a person is interested in finance, go to the Wharton School.

Now my boy thinks he wants to be a writer. Well, let him be a writer. He likes to write. That's all. Well, so let him write, then. Sometimes when you talk with the young fellows today you wonder why the hell they're even going to college. I was talking to a young fellow who married a relative of mine and I asked him what he was majoring in. And he says history. And I asked him if he was going to be a history teacher. He said no. Now he's working on a newspaper, and if he had taken up something about writing or advertising in college he'd have been all right.

Not only do young people seem to get mixed up about college, they can't seem to get straightened out when they start working on a job. Too many people can never stay in one place. They are always looking for two or three dollars more a week and they never get built up anywhere. I think too many people change their jobs too often. If they are with a good firm they should stay there and build themselves up. I don't believe in these people changing jobs every six months or every year. They never get any place. Because all you have to do is to look at a guy's record and you know something is wrong the way he flitted around here and there.

You can't go jumping around in jobs and still end up like me. If I hadn't had fifty years' experience in the watch business I might have panicked when I came to Gruen. After all, the situation reached the point where we were being sued by everybody. And there were times just before I arrived when they gave paychecks out on a Friday and said please don't cash them for a while, they might bounce. It got so bad they didn't have petty cash to pay the post office when the post office delivered packages. After being in business for more than eighty years, the company was on its way of going out of business.

When I took over they had a watch that was an insult to the name "watch." They had a watch with nineteen jewels in it, you would have been better off with a cheap one. Why, Timex was a better watch. They had a marvelous plant in Switzerland that could make wonderful goods, but it was losing a lot of money. When I came in I found we had a hundred thousand watches and movements in the Custom House and I won't tell you how much of that was good and how much was styled bad. Now, our plant is producing about three to four times as many watches as the day I come in to Gruen. That plant was operating at maybe twenty-five to thirty-five per cent of capacity and losing loads of money. It doesn't lose money any more.

It was a lot of hard work, but it was the fifty years of knowledge of being able to walk into a situation and put your finger on it and say this is what is wrong with your styling. This isn't something you can write down on paper, it is an intuitive feel of the thing. You've got to be able to look at your marketing situation throughout the country and see where you are weak and if it will take too long to repair the damage, then you've got to find another area to dispose of your merchandise.

But I was never nervous, no matter how bad it was. I never get nervous. That don't bother me. I was never frightened in my life. You just got to be able to see how stupid things could be corrected. And then you have to break in other people and that takes a long time. God Almighty, was it disorganized. Nobody knew what they were doing. Now Gruen is organized by stages. You've got each fellow doing his own work.

There is one thing. I like for people to do a good day's work. I don't want them to work overtime. And I want to be loyal to them. If a fellow is working out, you know that he ought to be getting a little bit more money. I always take care of all the people who work for me. And of course you cannot do this all by yourself. You must have certain people, three or four assistants, that you can trust to do their jobs. You tell them what you want done and they do it. You can't do everything yourself. That's silly, you know. You can't sell, you can't do this, you can't go out and chase all over for new dials. You have to have somebody do that. Or you can't write up catalogue pages. Or you can't do bookkeeping. You've got to have good people who keep your expenses, somebody who does your selling, and all. I've got a sign up in my office now that says, "Bad News From 1 to 2." Bad news only from those hours.

It's amazing how a company can get run down. Gruen started to go after the war. And then some fellows put some money together and they hired another president who didn't even live in New York. Things got so they had to sell a piece of machinery for meeting the payroll. The company wasn't dead entirely but it sure was dying.

But I want to tell you this. I will say the name Gruen was and is a terrific name and the watches were sold in the finest stores in America. High quality. And the movements they had back in those days were high quality movements.

But boy, when they started buying goods on the outside, people lost faith in the quality of the movement. And when you have a factory that the grass is growing around it and you got no help, it takes a long time to get things back to where you're making as much goods as we are today.

Our sales are up and we're beating our quota. We put up a quota this year of ten per cent more sales than last year. And we've passed that quota. Our factory is at one hundred per cent capacity and we are selling their full output and more. Things are looking up. Our profits are rising, too. I don't think about retiring much these days.

XI

In 1946, an engineer named H. E. Stumberg and his two sons, Louis, a mining engineer, and H. E., Jr., a geologist, founded Patio Foods, Inc., on a vegetable farm near San Antonio, Texas. The Stumbergs embarked on producing a quality frozen Mexican food line and today Patio Foods is the largest company in this field. Louis Stumberg is president of the company.

LOUIS STUMBERG

Somehow or other there's grown up in this country some pretty wild notions about Texans. We're all millionaires and we all made the money by complicated wheeling and dealing—no hard work, mind you—just a lot of big, complicated deals. Most of us, if you believe all those fanciful legends, simply went out into the back country, stuck a few drills into the ground and—bang, the next stop was Neiman-Marcus. Well, that's a lot of damned foolishness.

Few people that I know were successful without working like a dog and I'm no exception. Sure, I went out into the back country. But I was a kid fifteen years old, selling insurance off a bicycle. The insurance company gave me a country territory. I lived in a town of eight hundred people, and you can just figure what a country territory was. I rode around to these farmers and sold them a policy that I got ten dollars apiece to sell. In the Depression that thousand dollar policy was the only policy they had. That's all I ever knew about insurance. Selling insurance was one of my first jobs and I've been working ever since.

If you think I've got a formula for success, I'm afraid I'm going to disappoint you. Anybody that tells you there is a formula for success is wrong. The first thing you've got to do is to make up your mind that there's nothing more important in the world than being successful. And it doesn't mean that you have to be rich or anything else. It is a matter simply of satisfying yourself inside. No business is any more than that. Money was never the criteria of success for me. If, however, accomplishment is your criteria and you fail, then you say, "Well, I did my best, so I start over." Nobody wins every time. The biggest poker game a man ever devised is to be in business. Again and again you put everything you've got right on top of the table. Whenever you sit and sweat it out and worry about it instead of just doing it as good as you can and then moving on, then you'll never be successful.

If you let your past failures destroy your incentives or your push and drive, then you'll never be a success. Every failure should be just a step along the road—nothing else. Building a company takes the part of a child in your life. Our company is my child. When you start out it's a baby —it pukes, fills its britches, and it's a mess—it comes near dying again and again. At night you pace the floor with it and one day you see it take its first step. I'm not talking about having a fantastic idea that is so much better than anybody else's where it's clear from the start that the idea is going to be successful. The guy that comes up with this terrific idea is in the thin minority. Most businesses are not built on this great idea. Most of them come up with a good idea of how to do something that is already being done. But they do it better.

In our case, it so happens that we pioneered frozen Mexican foods and we were pioneers out of necessity. My dad was an electrical engineer, my brother was a geologist, and I was a mining engineer. In 1947, after the war, we all wanted to go into business together. We decided to go into something that none of us knew anything about, then we were all on an equal basis. It's not hard to understand why my dad, a man of sixty years old at the time, would make that kind of decision. My dad always believed in the individual. He said a man can do anything if he puts his mind to it. He taught us that man is never a failure until he admits it to himself. He may fail in certain instances, but he's not a failure until he sits down and says, "I am a failure," because as long as you're alive you have a chance to come back. My dad's been broke but he paid off every time. It might take him ten years. Each time he would go broke he said he learned something out of it, and he did.

We originally had gone into frozen foods to pack fruits and vegetables because it was a growing business, we felt, and looked like it had a good future. We located the plant in San Antonio in an irrigated growing district. Then the bottom dropped out of the frozen-food market. It turned out that we came into that field at the worst possible time that anyone could have. Right after the war frozen foods had gone to the very devil because of the poor packing done during the war.

Then came the moment of decision—what should we do? So we talked and examined the situation and, after about a month of discarding ideas, we finally came up with the notion of packaging frozen Mexican foods because San Antonio is the heartland of Mexican foods. I'll tell you, we started out with so little we damned near starved to death that first year. We had one desk in a small building and all three of us used the desk. We also had a woman who answered the telephone and typed out invoices. She used the desk, too. Pa said that if we didn't have a desk we wouldn't sit down so cotton-picking much. He said if you got corns on your rear instead of your feet, we'd never build the business.

My Dad and brother developed nearly all the formulas for the products. Pop's a fine cook and he's designed and built nearly all of the machinery in the plant. I just don't know what it cost us to go into operation, but we had very little money. When we finished putting up the first building you could have bought the whole thing at the end of twelve months for fifty cents on the dollar. I'll tell you we would have been glad to get out of it that year. My Dad is a square-headed Dutchman and my brother and I are the same way. Once we start something, we're going to stay with it—and we did.

We flipped a coin to see just who would travel and who'd be in the plant. It just so happened that I got the sales—or outside—end of the job because I wasn't married. My brother was. My brother and Dad ran the business and I traveled and sold.

You have no idea what it's like to start your own business unless you've gone through it. I'm going to tell you of some of my own experiences because I think you'll learn something from them—and I know the least you'll get out of it is that it's a mighty tough row to hoe.

I used to start work at five in the morning and quit at eight at night. My salary was six dollars a day and out of it I paid my car expenses, my meals, and my hotel. I would go out on the road to sell and not come back for four or five weeks at a time.

When you start your own business you've got to believe with all your might in your own product. Sometimes your belief leads you to do things as I did once in Dallas. I was calling on a food buyer and was showing him a package of frozen tamales. I really needed the business. He kidded me and kidded me when I told him how good they were, and he said, "I bet you could even eat those frozen."

I said, "Sure you can."

To make a long story short, I ate a whole dozen tamales that were half frozen. He gave me an order, and I barely made it out to the car because by that time I had the worst set of cramps from eating all that cold stuff. I lay on the back floorboard of my car for four hours. I was afraid to groan too loud because I was afraid someone would hear me and the buyer would learn about it and cancel the order.

Let me tell you I'm like the two sailors who were walking down the street and they spotted two gals hanging out a window. The gals said, "Come on up, boys, and we'll give you something you've never had."

And the sailors called back and said, "What, leprosy?"

Well, that's about the way it is with me. Leprosy is

about all I haven't experienced in the fifteen or sixteen years in building a company.

Any time one of my men starts giving me a song and dance, the odds are I've been through it. I know how a buyer can rip you from one end to the other. I know what it is to miss one sale right after another. I'm not interested in how he didn't do it. I'm interested in how he's going to do it.

And yet in all those years on the road I only lost my temper once. As I remarked earlier, some time after the company was formed, Dad suggested we flip a coin to see who would be what. It just so happens that I got the presidency and my brother got chairman of the board. That's about all it meant. I still didn't have anybody under me so it didn't matter. Anyhow, I walked into the office of a wholesaler in West Texas and he said, "You've been calling on one of my stores and selling direct instead of going through me. You bypassed me!" When I replied that I hadn't bypassed him, he said then it had been one of my men. I told him that I didn't have any man working out there. "Well, you're a liar," he said.

I'll take a lot of things but that's not one of them. A man calls me an S.O.B. or a liar he'd better be prepared to fight right there. "Mister," I said, "nobody calls me a liar and if you step outside I'll prove it."

He said, "I'll report you to your company."

"Mister, you're talking to the president, just start reporting," I told him.

"I won't buy from you any more," he said.

"I know you won't," I said. "You'll never buy from my company any more. Because I'll never ship you."

He then said he'd call up the head of his company to complain, but it so happened that the general manager of his firm was a personal friend of mine for many years and he knew I didn't lie. I called up the general manager right there in his office and I told him exactly what had happened. I told him I was very sorry but I would never ship this man again. I didn't care where he was located, but I would never, under any circumstances, ship him again. I would never call on him nor would any man from my company ever call on him. And furthermore if he'd step outside I would personally either beat the hell out of him or let him beat it out of me. The old boy at the end of the telephone apologized and said put the wholesaler on.

Whatever he said must have made an impression. Because the guy started apologizing when he hung up. I told him: "I don't want your apologies. I'll never speak to you again on the telephone or anywhere else because any man who will call a man a liar when he doesn't have all the facts is a fool." And to this day I have never done business with him.

Starting any new business is tough, but when you're dealing with an entirely new product—such as frozen Mexican foods—well, there were times when I thought it was impossible. I'd go to a grocery store and they'd look at me as if I were out of my mind. Frozen chili didn't even *sound* good, so you can see what we were up against. I'd go to a distributor and he would take me out to their warehouses and show me a bunch of stuff he had bought during the war. It was just sitting there and he was going to lose ninety cents on the dollar. And then he'd say, "And you want to sell me more?"

So I'd try the stores and work store by store, sometimes selling them two or three packages. When I was selling to the restaurants I'd be out at five in the morning showing a chef how to cook frozen tamales. A restaurant chef is busy by ten, which is why you have to see them early.

Lots of times I'd sit down at night in my hotel room and look in the mirror and go over every word that I'd said, trying to find out where I failed. Each failure is a step because each time I failed to sell I learned something about the man who turned me down. I learned what he didn't want.

Many a time I have walked through the warehouse of the distributor or buyer and looked at the merchandise he had. I had to convince myself that that man had actually bought something because my first impression when I was sitting at his desk was to say that the guy doesn't buy anything—all he can say is no.

But you find out that he didn't fail to buy—you failed to sell him. And I would say to myself, that man is buying millions of dollars' worth a year and I'll sell him. So I would try another approach. You have to keep sweating it out.

A man once told me years and years ago that the only secure man in this world is a man who is in jail. He's guaranteed a meal every time the bell rings and he has a place to sleep. When the going was really rough in those early days I'd ask myself a simple question: "Do I want to be secure and work until I am sixty-five and know I'll live in jail from the time I'm twenty?" The answer to me was, obviously, no.

All I want to preserve is the right of failure because if

you don't have the right of failure, you don't have the right to success. And you can't preserve the right of success without having been a partial failure someplace along the line. And most people today don't want failure. They can't accept a failure. They'd rather be like the Joneses who live next door to them than take a chance on failures.

Of course with all the problems I had on the road, I had a lot of nice experiences, too. You meet a few bad eggs, sure, but you meet a lot of fine people. One of the first men I ever called on was a man named Ed Abdo. He's a food buyer for Weingarten's in Houston and he's one of the biggest buyers in the South.

I went into his office and started to talk to him and he said, "Mr. Stumberg, have you ever sold before?" I told him no, that I was an engineer. Now here's one of the top men in the business and he took an hour to sit down and tell me what I should have done.

He said, "Now if you had told me all those things I'd have probably bought." And then he gave me an order. You talk about a lift that that talk gave to me. Because a man is kind enough to sit down and tell me what the score is.

I don't know how I can explain what real persistence is and how it's the difference between life and death to any young man starting out today. About the best example I can think of is one sale I made which took me two and a half years to finally make. I had an appointment with a fellow in Dallas and I was supposed to be there at eight-thirty.

A train had stopped me at a crossing and delayed me and I had showed up at eight-thirty-eight. Now who could figure that eight minutes would make that much difference? He looked up at me and said, "Mr. Stumberg, you're late, you're eight minutes late. That gives you exactly seven minutes to tell me anything you have to say." That was his greeting.

I put down the samples and said, "Mr. ——, in seven minutes I couldn't do this product justice, you justice, or myself justice—and all I would be doing would be wasting seven minutes. I'm going to give you back six of those minutes and I'll come back and call on you again when I can be more prompt." And I left the samples and walked out.

About two months later I came back. I called on that man every two months for two and a half years. I called on him so many times that he forgot whether I was a friend or an enemy. He just knew me by that time. I'd just walk in and talk to him. Sometimes I never even presented the items. I would just walk in and ask him if he had given any consideration to Mexican food and then I'd tell him what we were doing in the market and that I thought their company should be ready to buy. That's all, and I'd thank him for the interview and walk out. I never took the fifteen minutes he'd have set aside for me, usually just five or six.

Finally, one day, almost two and a half years after I met him, I walked in and said, "Joe, how are you?" (By this time it was Joe and Louis.) He said, "Fine, Louis, sit down." It was the first time he had ever said sit down.

All he said was: "Now just what items do you think we ought to put in?"

We spent some time discussing whether we should test

Patio Foods first. We decided to, and it subsequently sold well in the tests. And that was that.

Whenever I tell that story everyone assumes that the next thing I did was to go out and get roaring drunk. After all, what do you do after plugging for a sale for two and a half years? Actually, I don't drink. I sat down in the car for a long time and it was sort of a let-down. I mean I had sold everybody else. It's this competition that keeps you on your toes and when you finally get the hard one, it didn't mean half as much to me as the anticipation each time that I was there. Then I was interested only in the next sale.

In looking back over my part in the building of this company, I don't think now I'd go through it again. A man's a fool. What do you want to give up part of your life for? At the time, I had no regrets—don't misunderstand me. But if you're going to make a success of a business today you'd better learn plenty quick that you trade —and don't let anyone tell you that you don't.

What do you trade? You trade your home life, you trade your recreational life, you trade part of yourself. Every success is part of you. You trade part of yourself for accomplishment. Part of your guts, part of your thoughts, everything—that's what you trade. You're going to give up more things than anybody will ever know. Hours are going to pass into days, and weeks, and years, before you put an idea over. You're going to make this thing a success. That's all there is to it.

Now when it comes time to start your own business you're going to learn immediately that your government considers you an enemy. You're going to find out that most unions don't want excellence but mediocrity. They try to get the best man to conform to the poorest. Of course, this is wrong. I can tell you how to take a small stake and run it up into money. But I can't tell you how to combat the inroads that have been made to the incentive system. Just remember, your government preaches to the world for the incentive system and acts against it at home.

If you own a corporation, for over six months of the year you are working for the government, since the government takes fifty-two per cent of your profits, and that's in addition to the state taxes and everything else.

Despite these handicaps, it's still possible today to go out and make a success. If I were starting fresh today, the first thing I'd do would be to go into the yellow pages of my telephone book and see how many service industries are active in my town. Then, I'd sit down and make some calls to people and find out whether they are satisfied with their service in this particular field or that particular field.

The first thing to do is to find out the need or the place that you can cut out for yourself. Let's take the TV repair service, for example. Go to people. I'd even go house to house if necessary and talk to people and ask them if they are satisfied with the repairs they have been getting on their TV sets. And if you find out that a lot of them are unhappy, you know there is a need for your particular service. If I were going into the TV repair business, I would set up my shop—in my basement if necessary—and make these house-to-house calls within a radius around my shop and give people a certificate good for one free service call when they needed it. And by golly when they called me with that certificate, I would make damned sure they got good service. There's nothing better than showing people that you've got something they want.

I know the TV repair business sounds modest as hell, but I tell you, you can take really any business and build it up because so many people in these businesses today are not dedicated. You've got to be dedicated. If you give me a dedicated man, I'll tell you he can do a better job than a lot smarter man who isn't dedicated.

How far can a small business go? Obviously, it probably won't become nationwide. But what you can do is to build one business up as a vehicle to build another business. You can build up your capital and credit in one business to the point where you can go into another business. And so on.

The young man today couldn't set up a razor-blade business because it would probably cost twenty million dollars to get the thing going. You can't start out from scratch and start building cars unless you went in and built custom racing cars. But you *can* open up a repair shop and today many of the repair shops do shabby service. But you take a repair shop which is doing real good service, where the man owns it, and you'll find he's always got two or three mechanics who have a very personal interest in it and they're busy all the time. It's the personal touch in anything that is so important.

It's hard to compete with the well-established producing industries when you're starting out. It just takes too much of an investment. It's hard, or next to impossible, to go into the printing business with a small investment simply because of the enormous capital outlay you need for equipment and printing presses. But you could take a very small investment and set up a plant-cleaning operation. It would be a big opportunity. But the main thing a guy has got to do is to make up his mind not to be satisfied with mediocrity. Any time anybody is satisfied with being normal—he's wrong. He'd better go to work for the government or some big company where the norm is acceptable. Anybody that works cannot watch a time clock. He's going to have a rough road because he is in competition with men that *do* make success their primary concern and get ulcers and have heart attacks in their forties.

You ask me about success? Well, I firmly believe and maybe I'm wrong—but I firmly believe that nearly any of the service industries that I've mentioned—air-conditioning, TV repair—nearly any one of them can lead to success if a man went into it and really gave people good service and worked at it. You might have to ring doorbells at their houses to get their business.

The whole point of what I'm saying is get as close as possible to the consumer with as few middlemen in the way as possible. The distributor, the broker, wholesaler, and so on in many fields are going out because of direct selling. So you've got to get into this service business where you are in direct contact with the people that utilize your service. This is my thinking, anyhow.

If I were a young man, I think you could take a filling station and make money out of it by going and calling on people and selling them and by giving them a better wash job than the other man, or a better grease job. I'm telling you, you can take any service field because today so many services are being misused. But you've got to be dedicated. Hours cannot make any difference to you. You can be successful and it can be your own business, but the first step is to make up your mind that "I am going to be successful." By the same token you can make up your mind in that same direction and go to work for any company and probably be successful, too. But the fact is, most of the people today who start out are not prepared to make the sacrifice.

Conditions are changing in this country today. If you're a young man reading this, you've got to have that extra push. Most people let one or two or three failures discourage them or sour them on the whole thing. They say, "I'll go to work for somebody else and then I won't have this problem. Let Joe make the decision."

They don't want to make decisions. If you are in a position to make decisions you've got to be able to make up your mind to take the responsibility for those decisions. And this is what many people don't want to do. They'd rather pass the buck. You can't do it. You've got to get in that poker game and put your chips in the pot and play it as hard as you can and if the cards turn out that the other man beats you, you've got to play the next hand on its own merit.

You can't ever let up. You can take a lot of men in a poker game and snake-bite them twice and win every dollar they've got. Why can you bluff the other fellow? Because beating him twice legitimately you can bluff him the next time because he has lost confidence in his hand. He says it's luck. It isn't luck. Sure, there's luck involved in breaks. Everybody gets some breaks. It's taking advantage of those breaks when you do get them.

The Lord has been mighty kind to my brother, my Dad, and myself. He's given us opportunities; he's been overly generous. Without the help and confidence that you get from your religion, you'd give up many times. But dog-gone it, you've got to take advantage of those opportunities when they come. You always hear someone complaining, "If I just got a break." The guy may have fifty breaks but never recognized them when they came along.

You've got to have initiative. You've got to have that drive which tells you that you're going to be successful. I often think to myself of Israel. I'm not Jewish, but boy, they go over there to a little country and take a bunch of rocks and stuff that the Arabs would starve to death on and turn it into a nation. Sure, they had a lot of help. But they worked on their own. They worked!

In East Africa, the Indians were brought in to work on the railroads. Eventually, they controlled most of the commerce in East Africa. Why? Because they would work harder than anybody else. The natives didn't care. They didn't have initiative. But the Indians did. They had the urge to work and do things.

The same goes for the man who sits and waits for the order to be put on his desk. He's going to sit a long time. Or the guy who sits and waits for the television set to come in for repair just because he's put an ad in the back of the telephone directory. He's going to wait, too. I tell you, you can go in and do business immediately if you've got the guts to go out and ring doorbells and talk to people and explain what you are trying to do and live up to it. Never tell anybody anything that you are not willing to live up to.

You've got to be challenged to make a success in this world. I want to be challenged all the time. I want the challenge. I want the deep pit that I've got to crawl out of. I want the holes that I fall in now and then because it jolts me out of my complacency. I'm an introvert—the most insecure person you'll probably ever read about. And this is my whole secret of my being personally successful—insecurity. Because nothing ever satisfies me, I am insecure. As a result there's got to be more and more and better and better and you drive and drive to try to get this security. If I had been a secure person, it probably would be a different story.

My success has come from this nagging push all the time to prove to myself. I've got to prove to myself every day a dozen times that I can do it. A man's got to call me up and raise hell and threaten to quit doing business with me because of something my broker did and I've got to sell him and get him back. I need these challenges. I welcome them. I've got to beat my competitor every opportunity I get a chance. That's the reason when I am a failure, I'm driven on again and again and again. I can't recognize a failure, because once I do, I'm through. I'm nothing. I'm only as much as I am willing to work for and drive for.

I've had guys call me about a job and the first thing they ask me is, "What about your retirement plan?" I don't even talk to them. I'm not interested in what the retirement plan is. Our retirement is up in our brains. Our security is up there, too. My brain and my will to work—

they're my security. I don't want the government giving me a cradle-to-the-grave security. I don't want them giving me anything. I just want them to give me an opportunity. That's what gripes me so about things. The government keeps thinking that you want everything easy. I don't want it easy. I don't ask for it easy. I want an opportunity to prove that when the going gets tough I can still do it.

I'm not a cog in a machine—I'm an individual. I'm different from everybody else in this world. I may not be as smart, but then who is? There's always somebody smarter than the next man. I don't know what the answer is—but our government and everybody else seek to destroy everything that I believe in. Our competitors don't discourage me. The government discourages me because I see them trying to push everything down to the norm instead of stimulating people upwards.

A lot of kids today want to take the easy way out. They weren't brought up during the Depression. I got all of my insecurity from the Depression. I watched people go broke. I watched my Dad go broke. I watched all these things happen and that drive never left me. I don't want to go broke, but if I did, I think I could come back. I don't want Patio Foods to fail, but if it did I still think I could come back. I still think I've got enough guts to come back and not jump out the window. That's a coward's way out. It's the coward who takes the easy way out every time. Every time there's a fork in the road, one way is the easy and the other way is a little harder. You can judge a man by which side he takes. The rewards are so much better on this right road. Maybe not financially, but in yourself.

Who the hell do you have to answer to but your God and yourself? If you can't look yourself in the face every morning when you shave and be a little proud of what you've done, what can you do—what is there in this life but to feel that you did your best? I don't want a list of accomplishments. I'll be satisfied if they could just put one thing on my tombstone—"He did his best."

About the Author

CHARLES SOPKIN graduated from Emory University, Atlanta, Georgia, and the Columbia University Graduate School of Journalism. He has worked on the New York *Daily News,* the Atlanta *Constitution,* the Louisville *Times, Saturday Review,* and now is on the staff of *This Week Magazine.*